Heavenly Moments

COOKING WITH PHILADELPHIA* CREAM CHEESE

Kraft Kitchens

KRAFT
PHILADELPHIA
CREAM CHEESE

A LITTLE TASTE OF HEAVEN

Published in 2002 by
Hardie Grant Books
12 Claremont Street
South Yarra, Victoria 3141
Australia

ISBN 1-74064-089-6

Designed by Tanya Lea, The Marketing Store Worldwide, Melbourne
Art direction and editorial copy by Jane Wong, The Marketing Store Worldwide, Melbourne
Photography and styling by Adrian Lander and Kyle Barnett
Food styling by Linda Brushfield, Kraft Kitchens
Research, development and testing by Linda Brushfield and Kirsty Sands, Kraft Kitchens
Printed and bound in Singapore by Tien Wah Press

Heavenly Moments

COOKING WITH PHILADELPHIA* CREAM CHEESE

*Kraft Kitchens**

A LITTLE TASTE OF HEAVEN

contents

Smooth, creamy, white

Philadelphia Cream Cheese.

Heavenly.

Remember wriggling around, waiting to lick the spoon, while Mum made The Great Aussie Cheesecake? The thought of that creamy, rich mix of Philly on the back of a wooden spoon still unlocks a string of memories.

Dreamy sun-drenched summer days, birthday parties, Christmas gatherings, running through the sprinkler, chasing the dog — treasured times with your most favourite people. Cheesecake, and the smell of your grandmother's perfume. All Heavenly moments.

Everyone has grown up with Mum's favourite cheesecake recipes and, although we remember them with fondness, are they still a part of our lives? To some degree yes, and as we have grown up, Philadelphia has grown up too. In fact, Philly has outgrown the old cheesecake and French onion dip tag, and evolved into an ingredient that is as innovative as it is versatile – able to fill a huge range of cooking needs. Its stability and shelf life make it a fantastic product to keep on stand-by in the fridge, to extend recipes, or as a less expensive alternative to boutique gourmet produce such as goat's cheese or marscapone.

At less fat per serve than butter and margarine, Philly is a magnificent alternative for both spreading and cooking. So, rather than thinking of it as rich and heavy, you'll find it fills the spot in many recipes, leaving you with a lighter, healthier result. Even today's cheesecake recipes, refined by Kraft Kitchens, emerge as lighter and smoother than commercial cheesecakes. In baked items – although it is not an equal substitute for butter – Philly will provide a more moist result and you will find that they keep for longer. So, as well as adding great texture, it is ideal for mudcake-style desserts and can be incorporated into pastry too.

Flipping through the pages of this book you'll see exactly how many uses there are for Philadelphia Cream Cheese in both the block and spreadable varieties. You will also find recipes here provided by some of Australia's finest chefs. As an ingredient, you'll see it can be utilised in everything from fine dining through to mildly flavoured treats that kids will love. To its great advantage – unlike other soft cheeses – it can take on the flavours of our other ingredients and spices in both savoury and sweet recipes, whether used in its original form, or blended into a paste.

In every instance, the recipes in this book have been extensively tested by Kraft Kitchens and tasted by a team of enthusiasts until perfect results were achieved. We wanted to make sure that each dish was simple enough to prepare in the home kitchen, with ingredients that are generally available to most Australians. A broad range of tastes is covered and each recipe can be easily modified to your tastes. Where appropriate, tips and hints have been added. If you are stuck, or have any queries, you can reach the Kraft Kitchens team via the Kraft website, or by phone –

please see Philadelphia packs for details. We're sure that some of these dishes will become firm household favourites – your own modern classics to be remembered and enjoyed just as fondly by the next generation!

Where did it all begin? Where did Philly come from?

It all started in 1872, when Dairy Farmer Lawrence, of Chester, New York, set out to recreate the creamy French Neufchatel cheese. His moist, rich flavoured cheese was later distributed by C.D. Reynolds, who in 1880 began commercial production in his newly purchased Empire Cheese Company. The company passed through various hands and survived name changes until 1928, when it merged with Kraft USA, who raised the profile and consumption of Philly across the country.

Philly landed on our shores in 1956, the year of the Melbourne Olympics, and began production locally by The Kraft Walker company – the creators of Vegemite. In 1981, the tub of Philadelphia Spreadable joined the famous block in grocery stores across Australia. Subsequently, low-fat versions have been released to reflect our changing lifestyles.

So, what about the name?

In the late 1800s Americans perceived that Philadelphia produced the best quality foods in the country. The notion of a pure, wholesome and high-quality product was naturally a perfect fit with the Empire Cheese Company, so in naming their cheese Philadelphia they gave it another dimension, a character of its own.

This cheese that we still love today, is uncured and made from pasteurised cow's milk. It is gluten free, containing cream and salt, with vegetable gum added to the curd after the whey has been removed, following an 18 hour culturing process. It is more moist and stable than Neufchatel, and will keep in your fridge for up to 10 days after opening.

For best results, soften Philly before use. To soften Philadelphia block, remove Philly from foil. Roughly chop each block into 2.5cm cubes and place into a heatproof bowl. Microwave on high (800W) for 1 minute. Stir with a spoon until smooth.

Philly is so convenient and easy to use – enjoy!

brunch

BLUEBERRY PHILLY SNAILS

PREPARATION TIME: 15 MINUTES
COOKING TIME: 15 MINUTES
MAKES: 12

2 1/4 cups (280g) self-raising flour
  2 tablespoons caster sugar
    pinch salt
30g butter, chilled and chopped
  1 cup (250ml) milk (approximately)
125g PHILADELPHIA Spreadable Cream Cheese
    grated rind of 1 lemon
  1 punnet (150g) blueberries

GLAZE

1/2 cup lemon jam
  1 tablespoon water

SIFT the flour, sugar and salt into a large bowl. Rub in the butter until the mixture resembles coarse breadcrumbs. Stir in enough milk to form a sticky dough. Knead for 2 minutes on a lightly floured board until smooth.

ROLL the dough into a 30cm x 45cm rectangle. Combine Philly and lemon rind until smooth. Spread the lemon Philly mixture over the dough, and sprinkle with blueberries. Roll up from the long side (as for a Swiss roll) to enclose blueberries.

CUT the roll into 3cm slices and place cut slices side up on baking trays lined with baking paper. Bake at 200°C for 15 minutes or until golden. Brush with glaze.

GLAZE

COMBINE jam and water in small pan and stir over medium heat, until smooth.

PHILLY BIRCHER MUESLI

This muesli is not only healthy and refreshing, but the flavour is fantastic.

PREPARATION TIME: 10 MINUTES
REFRIGERATION TIME: 1 HOUR
SERVES: 2

  1 cup rolled oats
  1 cup (250ml) orange and mango juice
  2 red apples, grated
125g block Light PHILADELPHIA Cream Cheese, softened
1/2 cup (50g) hazelnuts, toasted and roughly chopped
1/2 teaspoon ground cinnamon
  1 punnet (150g) blueberries (fresh or frozen)
    extra apple slices, to serve
    fresh nectarine slices, to serve

COMBINE oats, juice and grated apple in a large bowl. Leave to soak for at least one hour, preferably overnight.

STIR through the Philly, hazelnuts and cinnamon. Spoon into serving bowls.

GARNISH with blueberries, extra apple slices and nectarine slices.

BLUEBERRY PHILLY SNAILS

PHILLY BIRCHER MUESLI

EGG AND BACON BLINIS

PREPARATION TIME: 25 MINUTES
COOKING TIME: 20 MINUTES
SERVES: 4

125g   block PHILADELPHIA Cream Cheese, softened
1   tablespoon maple syrup
1   cup (125g) self-raising flour
2   tablespoons sugar
1/4   teaspoon bicarbonate of soda
1   egg, lightly beaten
3/4   cup (185ml) milk
1   teaspoon lemon juice
30g   butter, melted
   butter – extra for greasing
4   eggs, for poaching
1   tablespoon vinegar
4   rashers rindless bacon, trimmed and cut in half
   maple syrup, extra to serve

COMBINE Philly and maple syrup in a small bowl and mix until smooth. Set aside.

SIFT flour, sugar and soda into a medium bowl. Make a well in the centre of the dry ingredients and add egg, milk, lemon juice and butter; whisk to form a smooth batter.

GREASE the base of a frying pan with the extra butter. When the butter bubbles, drop 1 1/2 tablespoons of mixture into the pan at a minimum of 2cm apart. When air bubbles form on top of blinis, turn and cook until well browned. Remove and keep warm. Repeat for remaining mixture, to make 8 blinis.

CRACK an egg into a cup, keeping the yolk intact. Bring a shallow saucepan of water and the vinegar to the boil. Stir around the edges of the pan with a wooden spoon in one direction to create a whirlpool. Carefully slip the egg into the middle, and gently simmer for 3–4 minutes, or until the yolk is soft-boiled. Remove with a slotted spoon and keep warm. Repeat for remaining eggs.

MEANWHILE, wipe out frying pan with paper towel. Add bacon and cook over medium heat until lightly crisp. Drain on paper towel.

ARRANGE two blinis on each serving plate. Spread blinis with Philly mixture. Top with bacon and an egg, then drizzle with extra maple syrup.

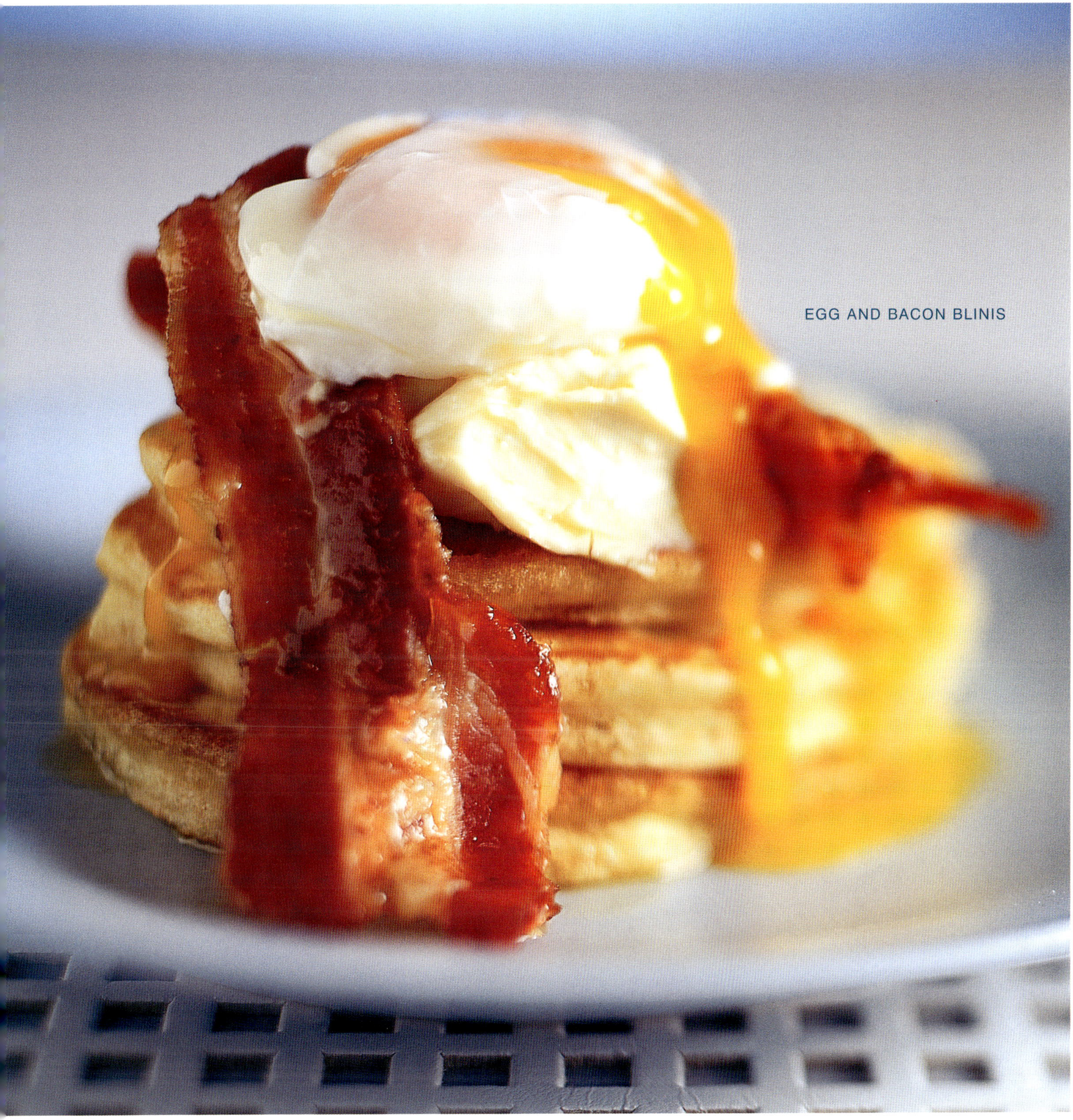
EGG AND BACON BLINIS

POACHED PEARS WITH ROSE WATER PHILLY BALLS

GRILLED PEACHES WITH MARSALA CREAM

POACHED PEARS WITH ROSE WATER PHILLY BALLS

PREPARATION TIME: 15 MINUTES
COOKING TIME: 45 MINUTES
SERVES: 4

250g block PHILADELPHIA Cream Cheese, softened
1 tablespoon honey
2 teaspoons rose water
4 firm pears
4 cardamom pods, bruised
4 whole cloves
1 cinnamon stick
   rind of 1 lemon
1/2 cup (110g) caster sugar
1/3 cup (60g) finely chopped shelled pistachio nuts
   dried rose petals for garnishing

COMBINE the Philly, honey and rose water in a small bowl. Chill for 10 minutes.

CUT the pears in half and place in a large saucepan with the cardamom pods, cloves, cinnamon stick, lemon rind and sugar. Just cover pears with water and gently simmer over low heat for about 30 minutes, or until cooked. Remove pears with a slotted spoon and reduce the liquid for about 15 minutes, or until thick and syrupy.

ROLL the Philly mixture into four even-sized balls and coat each with pistachios. Serve each Philly ball with two pear halves, drizzled with syrup.

GARNISH with dried rose petals if desired.

GRILLED PEACHES WITH MARSALA CREAM

PREPARATION TIME: 10 MINUTES
COOKING TIME: 5–8 MINUTES
SERVES: 4

250g block PHILADELPHIA Cream Cheese, softened
1 1/2 tablespoons caster sugar
1 1/2 tablespoons marsala
4 large slipstone peaches
1 tablespoon (20g) butter, melted
1/4 cup (45g) brown sugar, lightly packed
1/3 cup (60g) flaked almonds, toasted

COMBINE the Philly, caster sugar and marsala until smooth. Set aside.

CUT each peach in half and remove the stone. Brush the cut sides with butter and sprinkle with brown sugar. Place the peaches under a hot grill. Cook for 6–8 minutes, or until the peaches are hot and golden.

ARRANGE the peaches on serving plate. Sprinkle with the flaked almonds, and serve with a dollop of the marsala cream. Serve immediately.

SPICED APPLE MUFFINS

PREPARATION TIME: 15 MINUTES
COOKING TIME: 30 MINUTES
MAKES: 12

250g	block PHILADELPHIA Cream Cheese, softened
1/2	cup (90g) brown sugar, lightly packed
1	egg
1 1/4	cups (310ml) milk
1 3/4	cups (215g) self-raising flour
1	teaspoon ground cinnamon
1/4	teaspoon ground cloves
1/2	teaspoon ground nutmeg
1	cup canned pie apple
1/4	cup (55g) brown sugar, lightly packed, for sprinkling

LIGHTLY grease a 12 x 1/2 cup (125ml) capacity muffin pan.

COMBINE the Philly, brown sugar, egg and milk in a large bowl, and whisk until smooth. Sift dry ingredients and add with apples. Mix with a flat-bladed knife to combine. Do not over-mix, as it should retain its lumpiness. Spoon into prepared pan, and sprinkle with extra brown sugar.

BAKE at 200°C for 30 minutes, or until golden and cooked through. Serve warm or cold.

THREE CHEESE MUFFINS

PREPARATION TIME: 15 MINUTES
COOKING TIME: 15–20 MINUTES
MAKES: 12

250g	block PHILADELPHIA Cream Cheese, softened
1	egg
1 1/4	(310ml) cups milk
1 2/3	cups (200g) self-raising flour, sifted
50g	KRAFT Blue cheese, crumbled
1/2	cup (50g) KRAFT Grated Parmesan cheese
1/4	cup (25g) KRAFT Grated Parmesan cheese, for sprinkling

LIGHTLY grease a 12 x 1/2 cup (125ml) capacity muffin pan.

COMBINE the Philly, egg and milk in a large bowl, whisk until smooth. Add the sifted flour, blue and Parmesan cheeses. Mix with a flat-bladed knife to combine. Do not over-mix, as it should retain its lumpiness. Spoon into the prepared pan, and sprinkle with extra Parmesan.

BAKE at 200°C for 15–20 minutes or until cooked through. Serve warm or cold.

PUMPKIN AND BASIL MUFFINS

PREPARATION TIME: 15 MINUTES
COOKING TIME: 35–40 MINUTES
MAKES: 12

350g	pumpkin, peeled, cut into 1 1/2 cm cubes
1	teaspoon olive oil
250g	block PHILADELPHIA Cream Cheese, softened
1	egg
1 1/4	cups (310ml) milk
1 2/3	cups (200g) self-raising flour, sifted
1/4	teaspoon salt
1/2	cup (50g) KRAFT Grated Parmesan cheese
1/4	cup basil leaves, roughly torn
1/3	cup (35g) KRAFT Grated Parmesan cheese, for sprinkling

LIGHTLY grease a 12 x 1/2 cup (125ml) capacity muffin pan.

ON a baking tray, toss the pumpkin in oil to coat. Bake at 200°C for 20 minutes or until tender and golden.

WHISK the softened Philly, egg and milk in a large bowl. Add the flour, salt, Parmesan, basil and pumpkin. Mix with a flat-bladed knife to combine. Do not over-mix, as it should retain its lumpiness. Spoon into the prepared pan, and sprinkle with extra Parmesan.

BAKE at 200°C for 15–20 minutes or until golden and cooked through. Serve warm or cold.

SPICED APPLE MUFFINS
THREE CHEESE MUFFINS
PUMPKIN AND BASIL MUFFINS

LEMON AND PHILLY FRIANDS

LEMON BLINTZ

LEMON AND PHILLY FRIANDS

PREPARATION TIME: 20 MINUTES
COOKING TIME: 15–20 MINUTES
MAKES: 8

1 1/4 cups (155g) icing sugar
 1/3 cup (40g) plain flour
100g almond meal
      grated rind of 1 lemon
125g unsalted butter, melted
   4 egg whites

FILLING

250g block PHILADELPHIA Cream Cheese, softened
 1/4 cup (30g) icing sugar
      rind and juice of 1 lemon

SIFT the icing sugar and flour into a large bowl.
Stir in the almond meal, lemon rind and melted butter.

BEAT the egg whites with an electric mixer until stiff
peaks form. Gently fold beaten egg whites into the
cake batter. Spoon into 1/2 cup (125ml) capacity friand
or muffin tins and bake at 180°C for 15–20 minutes,
or until golden. Leave friands to rest in the pan for
5 minutes before turning them out onto a cake rack
to cool.

SLICE tops of friands not quite through and lift the top.
Spoon tablespoons of filling into the cut, and press lid
down lightly.

FILLING

COMBINE the Philly, icing sugar, lemon rind and juice
until smooth.

KRAFT KITCHENS HANDY HINTS

SERVE friands with Lemon Blintz syrup, if desired.

LEMON BLINTZ

PREPARATION TIME: 20 MINUTES
COOKING TIME: 30 MINUTES
SERVES: 4

   1 cup (125g) plain flour
   3 eggs, lightly beaten
   1 cup (250ml) milk
250g block PHILADELPHIA Cream Cheese, softened
250g cottage cheese
 1/2 cup (60g) sultanas
   2 tablespoons sugar
      grated rind and juice of 1 lemon
  60g butter
   2 tablespoons butter, for frying and for the syrup
   2 tablespoons sugar, for syrup

SIFT flour into a medium bowl. Make a well in the centre
and gradually whisk in combined eggs and milk until
smooth. Refrigerate batter for 30 minutes.

COMBINE Philly, cottage cheese, sultanas, sugar and
lemon rind until smooth.

MELT one teaspoon of the butter in a non-stick frying
pan. When it bubbles, pour 1/4 cup of the batter evenly
into pan. Cook pancake until lightly browned underneath,
then turn over and cook until golden. Repeat to make 8
thin pancakes.

SPOON two tablespoons of Philly mixture onto the centre
of each pancake. Fold in the sides of each pancake to form
a parcel. Add a further teaspoon of butter to the pan and
cook both sides of each parcel. Remove from pan and
set aside.

COMBINE remaining butter, lemon juice and extra sugar
in pan and simmer for 2 minutes. Serve syrup drizzled
over blintzes.

PARMESAN PESTO ROULADE

PREPARATION TIME: 25 MINUTES
COOKING TIME: 15–20 MINUTES
REFRIGERATION TIME: 2 HOURS
SERVES: 6

60g	butter
1/2	cup (60g) plain flour
2	cups (500ml) milk
4	eggs, separated
2	tablespoons KRAFT Grated Parmesan cheese
	salt and pepper, to taste
2	tablespoons KRAFT Grated Parmesan cheese,
	for sprinkling
250g	PHILADELPHIA Spreadable Cream Cheese, softened
1/2	cup chopped chives
2	tablespoons chopped basil
1/3	cup (50g) pinenuts, toasted
1/4	cup (40g) semi-sundried tomatoes,
	roughly chopped
	salt and pepper, to taste
100g	baby spinach leaves, wilted
1	red capsicum, roasted, thinly sliced

GREASE a 36cm x 25cm Swiss roll pan and line with baking paper. Melt the butter in medium saucepan, add the flour, and cook stirring, for 1 minute. Gradually stir in the milk, and stir continuously until sauce boils and thickens. Remove from heat, and stir in the egg yolks, Parmesan cheese, salt and pepper.

BEAT the egg whites in a medium bowl until stiff, and gently fold into the cheese mixture. Pour into the prepared pan, then sprinkle with extra Parmesan. Bake at 190°C for 12–15 minutes, or until set and golden. Turn out onto a clean tea towel. Carefully remove the paper and allow the sponge to cool completely.

COMBINE the Philly, herbs, pinenuts, tomatoes, salt and pepper in a bowl; mix well. Spread the Parmesan sponge with the Philly mixture. Top with a single layer of spinach, then red capsicum. Using a tea towel to assist, roll up the sponge from the short end (as for a Swiss Roll) to enclose the filling. Refrigerate roulade for at least 2 hours, allowing it to firm before serving.

PARMESAN PESTO ROULADE

SALMON MOUSSE

TALL TIMBERS, SMITHTON, TASMANIA

PREPARATION TIME: 20 MINUTES
COOKING TIME: 5 MINUTES
SERVES: 4

1/2	cup (125ml) fish stock
100g	fresh salmon fillet, skin removed
125g	block PHILADELPHIA Cream Cheese, cut into cubes
1/2	teaspoon horseradish cream
1/2	teaspoon salt
1/4	teaspoon black pepper
1/4	cup finely chopped chives
1	tablespoon finely chopped dill
2	teaspoons gelatine, dissolved in 2 tablespoons boiling water, cooled
1/2	cup (125ml) cream, lightly whipped salmon roe, optional, to garnish chives, to garnish thin wafer biscuits, to serve

HEAT the fish stock in a small saucepan to just below boiling point. Add the salmon fillet and poach over low heat for about 4 minutes, or until barely cooked. Remove salmon from the cooking liquid.

PLACE salmon, Philly, horseradish, salt and pepper in a food processor, and process until smooth. Stir in herbs and dissolved gelatine. Gently fold in the whipped cream.

SPOON into 4 x 1/2 cup (125ml) capacity moulds and refrigerate for several hours or until set.

GARNISH with salmon roe and extra chives. Serve with thin wafer biscuits.

MINI PHILLY FRITTATAS

PREPARATION TIME: 10–15 MINUTES
COOKING TIME: 15 MINUTES
MAKES: 24

250g	block PHILADELPHIA Cream Cheese, softened
1	small red onion, finely chopped
80g	baby spinach leaves, shredded
60g	hot salami, finely chopped
2	tablespoons plain flour salt and pepper
2	eggs, lightly beaten
24	(100g) semi-sundried tomatoes
1	tablespoon (20g) KRAFT Grated Parmesan cheese

GREASE two 12 x 20ml mini muffin pans.

COMBINE in a medium bowl the Philly, onion, spinach, salami, flour, salt and pepper. Mix well. Stir in beaten eggs and spoon into prepared pans.

TOP each muffin with one tomato and sprinkle with the Parmesan. Bake at 180°C for 15 minutes or until set and golden. Serve warm or cold.

SALMON MOUSSE

MINI PHILLY FRITTATAS

SEAFOOD GRATIN

SEAFOOD GRATIN

PREPARATION TIME: 20 MINUTES
COOKING TIME: 12–15 MINUTES
SERVES: 4

1/2 cup (125ml) white wine
1/2 cup (125ml) chicken stock
12 (250g) medium scallops
12 (250g) medium green prawns,
   peeled and deveined
250g block PHILADELPHIA Cream Cheese, softened
1 cup (155g) grated peeled potato
1/2 cup (125ml) cream
1 egg yolk
2 tablespoons chopped parsley
2 tablespoons chopped chives
1 teaspoon seeded mustard
   salt and pepper
2 cups (160g) roughly chopped fresh white bread
30g butter, melted
2 teaspoons grated lemon rind
   lemon, to garnish

BRING the wine and stock to the boil in a large frying pan. Add the seafood, reduce the heat and gently poach for about 3 minutes, or until just tender. Remove the seafood from the pan, then boil the cooking liquid until reduced by half.

COMBINE Philly, potato, cream, egg yolk, herbs, mustard, salt and pepper in a large bowl. Gradually add the reduced poaching liquid, then stir the mixture through the cooked seafood.

PLACE the bread, melted butter and lemon rind in a small bowl, and toss through to coat the bread. Spoon the seafood mix evenly between 4 x 1 cup (250ml) capacity ovenproof dishes. Top with the prepared bread. Bake at 180°C for 12–15 minutes, or until the bread is golden and gratin is hot and bubbly. Garnish with lemon. Serve immediately.

HERB TOMATO WITH CRISPY BACON

CIRCA, BRISBANE, QUEENSLAND

The left-over marinade can be used to marinate chargrilled vegetables or mixed with vinegar for an easy salad dressing.

PREPARATION TIME: 40 MINUTES PLUS
REFRIGERATION TIME: OVERNIGHT
COOKING TIME: 20 MINUTES
SERVES: 4

4 medium tomatoes
8 medium asparagus spears
8 rashers rindless bacon, trimmed and grilled until crisp

MARINADE

1½ cups (375ml) olive oil
8 golden shallots, halved
2 bay leaves
1 clove garlic, halved
1 tablespoon coriander seeds, crushed with back of a knife
1 teaspoon chopped thyme
1 teaspoon chopped coriander leaves
1 tablespoon chopped continental parsley
1 teaspoon cracked black pepper
½ cup (125ml) white balsamic vinegar
1 tablespoon honey
   juice of 1 lemon
   salt, to taste

FILLING

125g block PHILADELPHIA Cream Cheese, softened
1 tablespoon finely chopped chives
   salt and pepper, to taste
1 egg white

MARINADE

COMBINE the olive oil, shallots, bay leaves, garlic, coriander seeds, herbs and pepper in small pan and simmer over medium-low heat for 15 minutes. Remove from heat, stir in vinegar, honey, lemon juice and salt. Cool and transfer to a large bowl.

BRING a medium saucepan of salted water to the boil. Remove tomato cores with a sharp paring knife and plunge tomatoes into boiling water for 15 seconds. Remove and plunge into iced water to stop further cooking. Peel the tomatoes and use a teaspoon handle to remove seeds through the top hole. Add the tomatoes to the cooled marinade, cover and refrigerate at least 6–8 hours or preferably overnight for the best flavour.

FILLING

COMBINE Philly, chives, salt and pepper, and mix well. Beat the egg white with an electric mixer in a small bowl until soft peaks form. Add ⅓ of the beaten egg white to loosen the Philly mixture. Fold the remaining egg white into the Philly mixture until combined. Spoon into a piping bag fitted with a plain 7mm nozzle.

REMOVE tomatoes from the marinade, reserving the remaining marinade for garnishing. Fill the tomatoes with the Philly mixture by piping it in through the hole in the top.

BOIL, steam or microwave asparagus until tender and toss with marinade. Place the tomatoes on serving plates with the warm asparagus. Top with bacon and drizzle with marinade.

HERB TOMATO WITH CRISPY BACON

BROCCOLINI AND SWEET POTATO TIMBALES

PREPARATION TIME: 25 MINUTES
COOKING TIME: 25 MINUTES
SERVES: 6

1   medium (300g) sweet potato, peeled and cut into 1cm cubes
250g   block PHILADELPHIA Cream Cheese, softened
1   cup (250ml) cream
3   eggs, lightly beaten
    grated rind and juice of 1/3 lemon
1   bunch (200g) broccolini or broccoli flowerettes, chopped
1   tablespoon chopped fresh coriander
    salt and pepper
60g   butter
    sweet potato chips, to garnish
    broccolini, blanched, to garnish

LINE the bases of 6 x 1 cup (250ml) Texas muffin pans with baking paper.

BOIL, steam or microwave sweet potato until tender.

COMBINE Philly, cream, eggs, lemon rind and juice in a large bowl. Stir in the sweet potato, broccolini, coriander, salt and pepper. Spoon the mixture into the prepared pan. Bake at 160°C for 20–30 minutes or until set.

GENTLY run a knife around the outside of each timbale before removing from pan. Invert timbales onto serving plates and decorate with sweet potato chips and broccolini. Serve immediately.

KRAFT KITCHENS HANDY HINTS

To make crunchy sweet potato chips, slice the potato thinly and pan-fry over medium heat in a little butter and oil until golden brown and crisp.

MOROCCAN CHICKEN PARCELS

MOROCCAN CHICKEN PARCELS

PREPARATION TIME: 20–25 MINUTES
COOKING TIME: 30–35 MINUTES
MAKES: 4

1	tablespoon olive oil
300g	chicken breasts, cut into thin strips
1	large onion, chopped
2	cloves garlic, crushed
2	teaspoons grated ginger
2	teaspoons ground cumin
1	teaspoon ground turmeric
1/4	teaspoon ground cinnamon
1/4	cup (60ml) water
1/4	cup (30g) sultanas
1/4	cup chopped continental parsley
1	teaspoon grated lemon rind
250g	block PHILADELPHIA Cream Cheese, softened
50g	baby spinach leaves
8	sheets filo pastry
75g	butter, melted
	mango chutney and leafy greens, to serve

HEAT the oil in medium frying pan, add the chicken and cook for 5–7 minutes over medium heat until well browned. Add onion, garlic and spices and cook for a further 3–5 minutes or until onions are soft. Stir in water, sultanas, parsley and lemon rind and simmer for a further 2 minutes. Add Philly and spinach and stir until Philly is melted and combined.

BRUSH each filo pastry sheet with butter and divide into 4 pairs.

DIVIDE chicken mixture into 4 and spoon one quantity along one short end of each pair. Fold in edges and roll to enclose filling. Brush well with butter. Bake on greased baking tray at 180°C for 15–20 minutes or until golden. Serve hot or cold with mango chutney and leafy greens.

MEXICAN CHICKEN PIES

PREPARATION TIME: 20–30 MINUTES
COOKING TIME: 30 MINUTES
SERVES: 6

GUACAMOLE

1	large avocado, peeled and chopped
125g	block PHILADELPHIA Cream Cheese, softened
1	teaspoon lemon rind
1	teaspoon lemon juice
	salt and pepper, to taste
1	tablespoon KRAFT Mayonnaise

PIE

1	corn cob, peeled or 1 cup corn kernels, canned or frozen
1	tablespoon oil
300g	chicken breasts, diced
1	medium red onion, sliced
1 1/2	teaspoons ground cumin
1	teaspoon sweet paprika
1/2	teaspoon grated lime rind
	juice of 1 lime
2	tablespoons chopped coriander
1	tablespoon sweet chilli sauce
1/4	cup (60ml) water
6	tortillas, softened in the microwave
	fresh coriander leaves, to garnish

GUACAMOLE

BLEND the avocado, Philly, lemon rind and juice, seasonings and Mayonnaise until smooth; chill.

PIE

SPRINKLE the corn cob with water, wrap in cling wrap and microwave on high for 1 minute. Cut kernels from the cob with a sharp knife.

HEAT the oil in a medium-sized frying pan, add the chicken and cook for 5–7 minutes or until browned lightly. Add the onion and spices and cook a further 3–5 minutes until the onion is soft. Stir in the lemon rind and juice, coriander, chilli sauce, corn and water, and gently simmer for 5 minutes. Remove from heat and keep warm.

PUSH the tortillas into 6 x 1 cup (250ml) Texas muffin pans and bake at 180°C for 5–8 minutes or until crisp and golden on the edges. Spoon the hot filling into the tortilla cases and dollop with the guacamole. Garnish with coriander and serve hot or cold.

KRAFT KITCHENS HANDY HINTS

FOR a smoky, deeper flavour – barbecue or chargrill corn until soft (about 15–20 minutes).

TO soften tortillas, place them in the microwave on high for 1 minute or until soft.

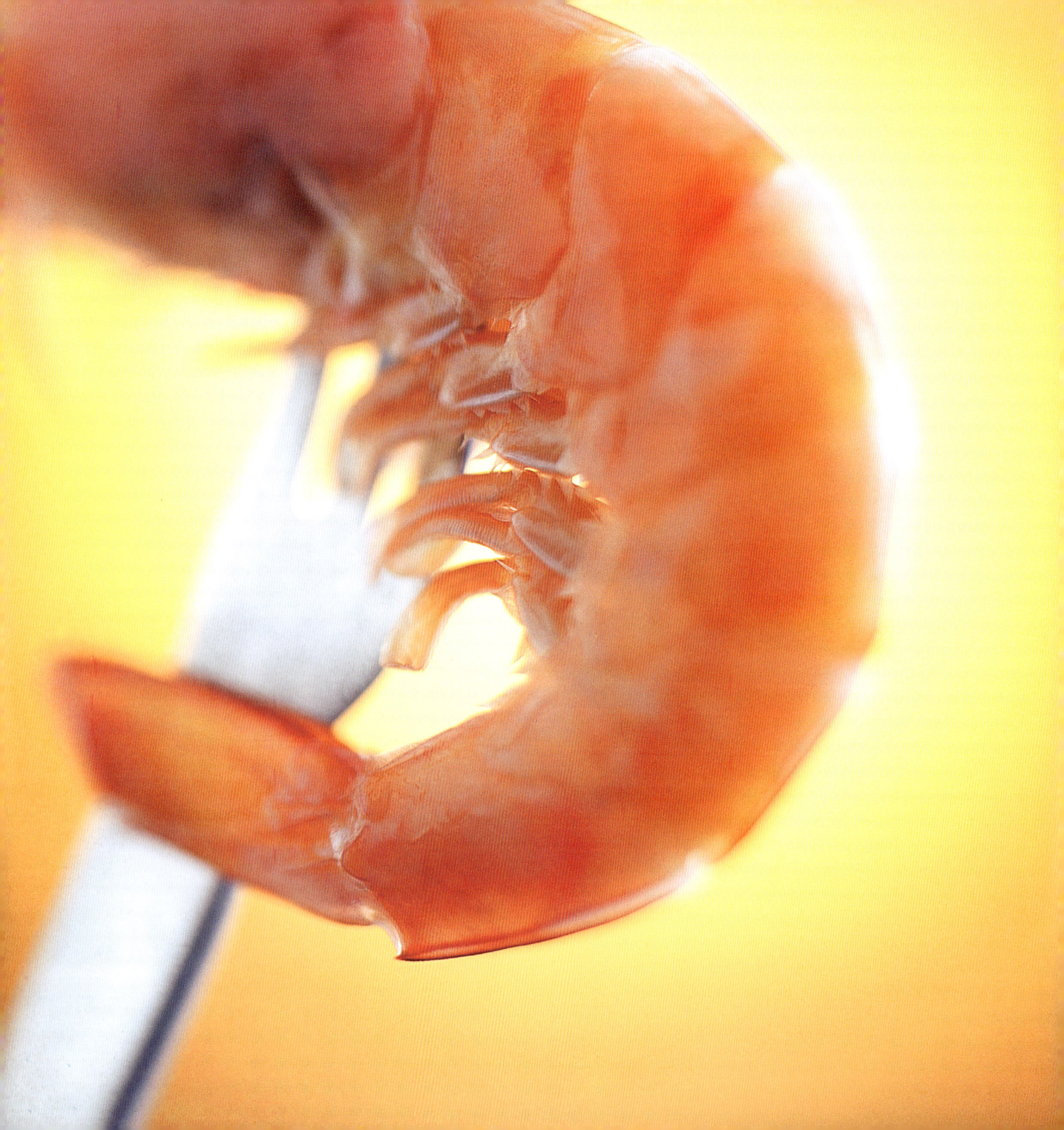

appetisers

SMOKED CHICKEN AND ALMOND DOLMADES

PREPARATION TIME: 20 MINUTES
COOKING TIME: 10 MINUTES
MAKES: 24

24 vine leaves, rinsed, patted dry, stems removed

FILLING

300g	smoked chicken breasts, chopped
250g	block PHILADELPHIA Cream Cheese, softened
1	tablespoon smoked almonds, roughly chopped
	grated rind and juice of 1 lemon
2	teaspoons chopped fresh chives
2	teaspoons chopped fresh parsley

DIPPING SAUCE

2	teaspoons cornflour
3/4	cup (185ml) chicken stock
1	egg, separated
	juice of 1/2 lemon
	salt and pepper, to taste

FILLING

COMBINE all ingredients in a bowl and mix well.

PLACE 1 tablespoon of filling at the base of each vine leaf. Fold the sides of leaf into the centre, and roll up to enclose filling. Serve with dipping sauce.

DIPPING SAUCE

BLEND cornflour with 2 tablespoons of cold stock, then combine with remaining stock in a small saucepan. Bring mixture to the boil, stir until thickened, and remove from heat. Whisk egg white in a small bowl until stiff peaks form. Add the egg yolk and whisk until combined. Whisk in lemon juice, then the stock mixture, in a thin stream until combined. Return to heat, and stir without boiling until slightly thickened. Season with salt and pepper.

SMOKED CHICKEN AND ALMOND DOLMADES

SMOKED SALMON BRUSCHETTA WITH DILL, CUCUMBER AND HORSERADISH

LA LINEA, ST KILDA, VICTORIA

PREPARATION TIME: 30 MINUTES
REFRIGERATION TIME: 30 MINUTES
SERVES: 8

1/3   continental cucumber, peeled, seeded and finely diced
     coarse cooking salt
250g   block PHILADELPHIA Cream Cheese, softened
2   tablespoons finely chopped fresh dill
     rind and juice of half a lemon
1   tablespoon horseradish cream
8   slices ciabatta bread
1   tablespoon virgin olive oil
1   clove garlic, halved
8   slices (100g) smoked salmon
     fresh dill, extra, to garnish
     cracked pepper, to taste
     lemon rind, to garnish

SPRINKLE diced cucumber liberally with salt and leave for 20 minutes to extract excess water. Wash thoroughly and pat dry with paper towel.

COMBINE Philly, dill, lemon rind and juice, and horseradish cream. Stir in cucumber and refrigerate for 30 minutes or until firm.

PREHEAT a grill pan over medium heat until hot. Brush bread with olive oil and chargrill on both sides until golden. Rub top of bread with the cut side of the garlic clove.

PLACE a generous spoonful of mousse on each bread slice. Top with a slice of smoked salmon, extra dill, cracked pepper, and lemon rind.

SMOKED SALMON BRUSCHETTA WITH
DILL, CUCUMBER AND HORSERADISH

FILLED WITLOF LEAVES

SEARED SCALLOP TOASTS

OLIVE AND TOMATO CHECKERBOARDS

CUCUMBER ROLLS

FILLED WITLOF LEAVES

PREPARATION TIME: 20 MINUTES
COOKING TIME: 5–10 MINUTES
MAKES: 24

125g   block PHILADELPHIA Cream Cheese, softened
50g   KRAFT Blue Cheese
1/4   cup (35g) shelled pistachio nuts,
        roughly chopped
2   red apples, cut into thin wedges
1/3   cup (60g) brown sugar, lightly packed
6   slices (100g) prosciutto, thinly sliced
24   large witlof leaves
      thin wafer biscuits, to serve

COMBINE Philly and Blue Cheese in a small bowl and mix
until smooth. Stir in the pistachio nuts.

HEAT a large, greased frying pan over medium heat. Add the
apples and sprinkle with sugar. Cook, stirring occasionally,
for 3–5 minutes until the sugar is melted and the apples
are caramelised.

COOK prosciutto in a small frying pan over medium heat
until crisp. Drain on paper towel.

SPOON the cheese mixture evenly onto witlof leaves,
top with apple and prosciutto. Serve with thin wafer biscuits.

SEARED SCALLOP TOASTS

PREPARATION TIME: 20 MINUTES
COOKING TIME: 10–15 MINUTES
MAKES: 30

1   bread stick cut into 30 thin slices
      garlic and butter cooking spray
250g   block PHILADELPHIA Cream Cheese, softened
2   tablespoons lemon juice
1 1/2   tablespoons KRAFT Mayonnaise
1   tablespoon chopped capers
1   tablespoon finely chopped chives
1   tablespoon finely chopped dill
2   teaspoons grated lemon rind
      salt and pepper, to taste
1   medium red capsicum, roasted and thinly sliced
30   large (700g) scallops
      fresh dill sprigs, to garnish
      baby capers, to garnish

SPRAY the bread slices on both sides with garlic and
butter spray. Heat a chargrill pan over medium-high heat
until hot, and grill both sides of the bread until golden.

COMBINE Philly, lemon juice, Mayonnaise, capers, herbs,
lemon rind, salt and pepper in a small bowl and stir until
combined. Spread Philly mixture on toasts and top with
red pepper.

PREHEAT the chargrill pan over medium-high heat until
hot. Spray scallops with garlic and butter spray, then sear
both sides in the pan. Remove when cooked and place one
scallop on each piece of toast. Garnish with dill sprigs and
baby capers. Serve immediately.

OLIVE AND TOMATO CHECKERBOARDS

PREPARATION TIME: 1 HOUR
COOKING TIME: 35 MINUTES
MAKES: 16

16 cherry tomatoes, halved
1 tablespoon olive oil
1 tablespoon balsamic vinegar
1/2 teaspoon sugar
salt and pepper, to taste
90g butter, chilled and cubed
1 cup (125g) plain flour
1 cup (125g) grated mature tasty cheese
125g block PHILADELPHIA Cream Cheese, softened
1/2 teaspoon cayenne pepper
16 black olives, pitted and halved
sprigs of thyme for garnish

COMBINE tomatoes with oil, vinegar, sugar, salt and pepper in a small bowl; mix well. Place tomatoes in a single layer on baking tray and bake at 160°C for 20 minutes or until tomatoes are slightly shrivelled and soft.

PLACE butter and flour in a food processor and process until mixture resembles breadcrumbs. Add cheese and process until the dough forms a ball. Wrap dough in plastic wrap and refrigerate until firm.

ROLL out the dough between two pieces of baking paper to a 7mm thickness. Cut into 5 cm squares; chill until firm. Place on greased baking trays and bake at 180°C for 15 minutes, or until crisp and golden.

COMBINE Philly and cayenne pepper. Spread biscuits with the Philly mixture, then top each biscuit with two tomato halves, two olive halves, and a sprig of thyme.

CUCUMBER ROLLS

PREPARATION TIME: 30–40 MINUTES
REFRIGERATION TIME: 20 MINUTES
MAKES: 24

2 large continental cucumbers
250g block PHILADELPHIA Cream Cheese, softened
2 teaspoons horseradish cream
2 teaspoons finely chopped fresh dill
2 teaspoons finely chopped fresh chives
grated rind of 1 lemon
300g thinly sliced ham, smoked salmon or rare roast beef
1 small red capsicum, finely sliced into 5cm lengths, or
1 punnet snow pea sprouts, trimmed to 5cm lengths
fresh dill sprigs, to garnish
salt and pepper, to taste

USING a vegetable peeler, slice along the length of the cucumbers to give 24 slices. Pat the slices dry on paper towel.

COMBINE Philly, horseradish cream, herbs and lemon rind in a small bowl. Spread 2 teaspoons of the mixture over each cucumber slice (it will be slippery at first). Top the slices with meat – or smoked salmon – and trim to fit. Place bundles of red capsicum – or snow pea sprouts – at one end of each slice. Roll up cucumber to enclose the filling. Stand upright and refrigerate for 20 minutes until filling is firm. Garnish with dill sprigs and season with salt and pepper, if desired.

KRAFT KITCHENS HANDY HINTS

FOR that extra special touch: wrap an extra piece of meat or smoked salmon around the cucumber roll and secure with a toothpick. Sprinkle with extra salt and pepper.

BAKED SHALLOT TART
WITH PHILLY

THE POINT, ALBERT PARK, VICTORIA

PREPARATION TIME: 20 MINUTES
COOKING TIME: 40–50 MINUTES
SERVES: 4

1	sheet frozen puff pastry
32	medium golden shallots, peeled
50g	butter, melted
50g	caster sugar
	salt and pepper, to taste
125g	block PHILADELPHIA Cream Cheese, softened
50g	baby rocket leaves
	crisp garden salad, to serve

USING a 10cm round cutter, cut four circles from the pastry sheet. Pierce the pastry with a fork and bake at 200°C for 8–10 minutes or until golden.

TOSS the shallots with butter and sugar in a baking dish. Bake at 180°C for 30–40 minutes until shallots are soft and caramelised; season with salt and pepper.

SPREAD the cooked pastry circles with Philly and then top with shallots and baby rocket. Drizzle the tart with any remaining pan juices. Serve with a crisp garden salad.

KRAFT KITCHENS HANDY HINT

BLANCHING shallots (and onions) in boiling water makes them easier to peel.

BAKED SHALLOT TART
WITH PHILLY

BEETROOT DIP

This lovely pink coloured dip will make a spectacular addition to your next dip platter.

PREPARATION TIME: 10 MINUTES
REFRIGERATION TIME: 30 MINUTES
MAKES: 3 CUPS

425g	can whole beetroot, drained
250g	block Light PHILADELPHIA Cream Cheese
1/4	cup finely chopped chives
1	tablespoon lemon juice

FINELY chop one beet and set aside. Combine the remaining beetroot, Philly, chives and juice in a food processor and process until smooth.

FOLD in the reserved chopped beet and refrigerate for at least 30 minutes. Serve with lean meats or use as a dip with crunchy bread and crudites.

BEETROOT DIP

THAI BAKED PHILLY

Simple and stylish, this dip is fantastic for friends that drop by. It's sure to become a firm favourite.

PREPARATION TIME: 5 MINUTES
COOKING TIME: 10 MINUTES
SERVES: 4

250g block PHILADELPHIA Cream Cheese
 1/3 cup sweet chilli sauce
 1/4 cup roughly chopped fresh coriander
       rice crackers or grissini sticks, to serve

PLACE one whole Philly block on a baking tray, lined with baking paper. Pour over chilli sauce to cover.

BAKE at 180°C for 10 minutes. Sprinkle with coriander and serve with rice crackers or grissini sticks.

THAI BAKED PHILLY

THAI SAUSAGE ROLLS

PREPARATION TIME: 20 MINUTES
COOKING TIME: 15–20 MINUTES
MAKES: 32

500g   chicken mince
125g   block PHILADELPHIA Cream Cheese, softened
   1   medium carrot, grated
   1   medium red onion, finely chopped
   2   tablespoons sweet chilli sauce
   1   tablespoon green curry paste
   4   sheets frozen puff pastry, thawed
   1   egg, beaten
   2   tablespoons sesame seeds, for sprinkling
       sweet chilli sauce, for dipping

COMBINE mince, Philly, carrot, onion, chilli sauce and curry paste in a medium bowl and mix well.

CUT each pastry sheet in half. Spoon 4 tablespoons of mince mixture along one long edge of each pastry sheet. Brush the opposite edge with egg and fold pastry over to enclose filling. Lightly press edges together to seal. Brush with egg and sprinkle with sesame seeds. Trim each end and cut each roll into two. Place rolls on greased baking trays.

BAKE at 200ºC for 15–20 minutes or until mince is cooked and pastry is crisp and golden. Serve hot with chilli sauce on the side.

MINI CORN AND CRAB CAKES

PREPARATION TIME: 30 MINUTES
REFRIGERATION TIME: 45 MINUTES
COOKING TIME: 5 MINUTES
MAKES: 24

125g block PHILADELPHIA Cream Cheese, softened
   2 cloves garlic, crushed
   1 tablespoon sweet chilli sauce
   1 tablespoon caster sugar
   2 teaspoons finely grated ginger
   1 teaspoon fish sauce
      pinch salt
 3/4 cup (60g) fresh white breadcrumbs
170g can crab meat, drained
 1/2 cup (100g) fresh, canned, or frozen corn kernels
 1/2 cup (90g) water chestnuts, chopped
   3 spring onions, thinly sliced
 3/4 cup (60g) fresh white breadcrumbs, extra
   1 tablespoon sesame seeds
   1 tablespoon plain flour
      peanut oil, for deep frying

COMBINE Philly, garlic, chilli sauce, sugar, ginger, fish sauce and salt in a small bowl, mixing well. Stir in the breadcrumbs, crab meat, corn, water chestnuts and spring onions. Chill for 30 minutes.

COMBINE the extra breadcrumbs, sesame seeds and flour in a small bowl. Roll tablespoons of Philly mixture into bite-sized balls and roll in breadcrumb mixture to coat. Chill for 15 minutes.

HEAT the oil in a deep saucepan. Deep-fry crab cakes in oil, in batches, until golden. Remove from oil and drain well on paper towel; serve immediately.

TROUT AND WASABI PASTRIES

PREPARATION TIME: 30 MINUTES
COOKING TIME: 15 MINUTES
MAKES: 24

   1 sheet frozen puff pastry
   1 teaspoon chilli oil
   1 medium whole smoked trout, skin and flesh
      removed or 180g smoked trout fillets
      Vietnamese mint leaves
      or coriander
      lime wedges, to garnish

BRUSH the pastry evenly with chilli oil until coated. Prick the pastry all over with a fork. Cut into 24 squares. Bake at 180°C for 15 minutes or until golden.

SPREAD the cooked pastry with wasabi cream. Top with pieces of trout, and garnish with mint and lime wedges.

WASABI CREAM

250g block PHILADELPHIA Cream Cheese, softened
      grated rind and juice of 1 lime
 1 1/2 teaspoons prepared wasabi paste
      salt and pepper, to taste

WASABI CREAM

COMBINE all ingredients until smooth.

MINI CORN AND CRAB CAKES

TROUT AND WASABI PASTRIES

PANCETTA AND ROCKET PIZZA

RAGAZZI, MIDDLE PARK, VICTORIA

PREPARATION TIME: 5 MINUTES
COOKING TIME: 15 MINUTES
SERVES: 2

20cm	pizza base
2	tablespoons (50g) tomato paste
1	tablespoon basil pesto
250g	block PHILADELPHIA Cream Cheese, softened
8	slices pancetta
50g	semi-sundried tomatoes
45g	baby rocket leaves

SPREAD the pizza base evenly with combined tomato paste, pesto and Philly. Top with pancetta, semi-sundried tomatoes and rocket leaves.

BAKE at 180ºC for 10–15 minutes or until the base has browned and the pancetta is crisp and browned.

PANCETTA AND ROCKET PIZZA

SMOKED SALMON PIZZA

RAGAZZI, MIDDLE PARK, VICTORIA

PREPARATION TIME: 5 MINUTES
COOKING TIME: 15 MINUTES
SERVES: 2

20cm	pizza base
2	tablespoons (50g) tomato paste
250g	block PHILADELPHIA Cream Cheese, cubed
8	slices (100g) smoked salmon
1	Spanish onion, sliced
2	tablespoons capers
1	tablespoon olive oil

SPREAD the pizza base evenly with tomato paste. Top with cubed Philly.

TOP with smoked salmon, spanish onion and capers and drizzle with olive oil. Bake at 180°C for 10–15 minutes or until base has browned and Philly is golden brown.

SMOKED SALMON PIZZA

LEEK, ASPARAGUS AND
SMOKED SALMON TERRINE

PREPARATION TIME: 30 MINUTES
COOKING TIME: 5 MINUTES
SERVES: 4–6

1   bunch (10) thin asparagus, trimmed to
    fit the length of the pan
2   large and long leeks
1   tablespoon (20g) butter
2   250g blocks PHILADELPHIA Cream Cheese, softened
100g   smoked salmon, finely chopped
    grated rind and juice of $1/2$ lemon
1   tablespoon horseradish
    salt and pepper, to taste

BLANCH the asparagus in boiling water for 2–3 minutes, until bright green and just tender. Remove and plunge into cold water; drain well.

FINELY chop the white section of the leeks, to give 1 cup. Slice the green section lengthwise into long ribbons. Blanch in boiling water for 1–2 minutes or until softened, then plunge into cold water; drain well.

MELT the butter in a large pan, add white leeks and cook for 2 minutes, or until softened; cool. Combine with the Philly, salmon, lemon rind and juice, horseradish, and seasonings in a large bowl until combined.

LINE an 11cm x 21cm loaf pan with plastic wrap. Layer the leek ribbons across the pan ensuring that they overlap by 1 cm. Spoon half the Philly mixture evenly into the pan, top with the asparagus spears, then spoon in the remaining Philly. Fold the leek ends over the filling to enclose; trim if necessary. Chill until firm. Invert onto a serving plate and serve sliced.

LEEK, ASPARAGUS AND SMOKED SALMON TERRINE

dinner

HERBED RAVIOLI WITH SAFFRON PRAWN SAUCE

PREPARATION TIME: 20 MINUTES
COOKING TIME: 10 MINUTES
SERVES: 4

250g block PHILADELPHIA Cream Cheese, softened
250g firm white boneless fish fillets
 1/4 cup (20g) fresh breadcrumbs
      grated rind of 1 lemon
  2   teaspoons finely chopped parsley
  2   teaspoons finely chopped chives
  2   teaspoons finely chopped dill
      salt and pepper to taste
 60   (300g) wonton wrappers

PRAWN SAUCE

  1   cup (250ml) white wine
  1   cup (250ml) chicken, fish or vegetable stock
 10   saffron threads
 1/2 cup (125ml) cream
  1   teaspoon cornflour, blended with 2 tablespoons
      of cold water
 12   (250g) green prawns, shelled and deveined
      with tails left intact

COMBINE the Philly, fish, breadcrumbs, lemon rind, herbs, salt and pepper in a food processor. Process until smooth.

PLACE tablespoons of the Philly mixture in the centre of half the wonton wrappers. Brush edges with water and top with a second wrapper; press edges to seal together.

ADD the ravioli to a large pan of boiling water; boil uncovered for about 6 minutes or until tender. Drain, and serve ravioli drizzled with Prawn Sauce.

PRAWN SAUCE

COMBINE white wine, stock and saffron in a medium-sized pan over medium heat. Bring to the boil and simmer until reduced by half. Stir in the cream and blended cornflour; simmer until slightly thickened. Add the shelled prawns and simmer a further 5 minutes or until the prawns are just tender.

HERBED RAVIOLI WITH
SAFFRON PRAWN SAUCE

CHICKEN WITH SALSA VERDE

CHICKEN WITH SALSA VERDE

PREPARATION TIME: 15 MINUTES
COOKING TIME: 25 MINUTES
SERVES: 4

  4   chicken breasts (500g), trimmed
  2   tablespoons finely chopped parsley
  2   tablespoons roughly chopped capers
  4   anchovies, roughly chopped
      salt and pepper, to taste
250g block PHILADELPHIA Cream Cheese, softened
  8   baby spinach leaves
 30g butter
  1   tablespoon oil

SALSA VERDE

 1/4 cup (60ml) olive oil
  1   tablespoon white wine vinegar
  3   anchovies, finely chopped
  1   clove garlic, crushed
  2   tablespoons finely chopped parsley
  2   tablespoons finely chopped basil
  1   tablespoon finely chopped green olives
  1   tablespoon capers, finely chopped
  1   tablespoon finely chopped gherkins
      salt and pepper

CUT an 8–10cm long deep slit in one side of each chicken fillet to form a pocket. Fold the parsley, capers, anchovies, salt and pepper into the Philly, until well combined.

STUFF each chicken breast with 1/4 of the Philly mixture and top with spinach leaves. Close, sealing with toothpicks.

HEAT the butter and oil in a large frying pan over high heat. Add the chicken and cook for 2 minutes each side, or until well browned. Transfer chicken to a baking tray and bake at 180°C for about 20 minutes, or until chicken is tender. Serve hot or cold with Salsa Verde.

SALSA VERDE

COMBINE all ingredients in a small bowl; mix well. Serve drizzled over chicken.

ROASTED VEGETABLE SKEWERS WITH WHITE BEAN DIP

PREPARATION TIME: 15 MINUTES
COOKING TIME: 30 MINUTES
SERVES: 4

8	25cm bamboo or metal skewers
400g	sweet potatoes
400g	parsnips
400g	potatoes
1/3	cup finely chopped dill
2	tablespoons olive oil
2	teaspoons ground cumin
1/4	teaspoon ground coriander
	salt and pepper, to taste

WHITE BEAN DIP

400g	can butter beans (cannellini), drained
125g	PHILADELPHIA Spreadable Cream Cheese
1	clove garlic, crushed
1	tablespoon lemon juice
1	tablespoon olive oil
	salt and pepper, to taste

SOAK bamboo skewers in water for 10 minutes. This will prevent them from burning when roasting.

PEEL and cut vegetables into 2cm cubes. Steam or microwave vegetables for 5 minutes to soften. Thread alternate pieces of vegetable onto skewers and place on a greased baking tray.

COMBINE dill, oil, spices, salt and pepper in a small bowl and mix well. Brush vegetables liberally with the seasoned oil mixture. Roast at 200°C for 15 minutes. Turn skewers over and bake for a further 15 minutes, or until crispy. Serve with dip.

WHITE BEAN DIP

JUST before serving, place all ingredients in food processor and process until smooth.

LENTIL PATTIES WITH TOMATO SAUCE

PREPARATION TIME: 15 MINUTES
COOKING TIME: 15–20 MINUTES
SERVES: 4

125g	block PHILADELPHIA Cream Cheese, softened
400g	can lentils, drained and rinsed
1	medium carrot, grated
1/2	medium onion, finely chopped
2	cloves garlic, crushed
	grated rind of 1/2 lemon
	plain flour for dusting
1	tablespoon olive oil

TOMATO SAUCE

1	tablespoon olive oil
1/2	medium onion, finely chopped
400g	can diced tomatoes
1	tablespoon tomato paste
125g	block PHILADELPHIA Cream Cheese, softened
1	tablespoon finely chopped coriander
1/2	teaspoon ground cumin
1/2	teaspoon sugar

COMBINE Philly, lentils, carrot, onion, garlic and lemon rind in a bowl, and mix until combined. Shape mixture into 8 patties and roll in flour, shaking away any excess flour.

HEAT the oil in large frying pan and cook the patties over medium heat for about 5 minutes each side, or until golden and heated through. Serve with the tomato sauce.

TOMATO SAUCE

HEAT the oil in saucepan and cook onion over medium heat for 3–5 minutes, or until translucent. Add the undrained tomatoes and tomato paste. Simmer for 5 minutes, or until the mixture is reduced and thickened. Stir in remaining ingredients until combined; heat through.

ROASTED VEGETABLE SKEWERS
WITH WHITE BEAN DIP

LENTIL PATTIES WITH TOMATO SAUCE

CREAM CHEESE AND SMOKED TROUT PASTA

*FRANGOS & FRANGOS,
DAYLESFORD, VICTORIA*

**PREPARATION TIME: 20 MINUTES
COOKING TIME: 15 MINUTES
SERVES: 4**

250g	block PHILADELPHIA Cream Cheese, softened
1	cup (250ml) sour cream
80g	butter, softened
	rind and juice of 2 lemons
375g	pappardelle or fettucine pasta
	pinch salt
50g	butter for the pan
2	cloves garlic, crushed
200g	sliced smoked trout
2	tablespoons finely chopped dill
2	tablespoons finely chopped parsley
1	tablespoon capers

COMBINE the Philly, sour cream, butter, lemon rind and juice in a bowl over a pan of simmering water. Whisk until the mixture is smooth and light.

ADD the pasta to a large saucepan of salted boiling water. Cook until al dente. Drain pasta and set aside.

MELT the extra butter in a saucepan, add garlic and cook, stirring for one minute without browning. Add the cooked pasta, half the Philly mixture, half each of the trout, herbs and capers. Toss well to combine.

SPOON into serving bowls and top with dollops of Philly mixture, remaining trout, herbs and capers.

CREAM CHEESE AND SMOKED TROUT PASTA

PHILLY GNOCCHI

PREPARATION TIME: 20 MINUTES
COOKING TIME: 30–35 MINUTES
SERVES: 4

3	medium (700g) Desiree potatoes
125g	block PHILADELPHIA Cream Cheese, softened
1/2	cup (60g) plain flour
1	egg
1/4	cup finely chopped chives
1/2	cup finely chopped parsley
	salt and pepper to taste
	extra flour, for rolling
2	large (160g) mushrooms (e.g. Swiss brown or field), sliced
2	large slices prosciutto
1/2	cup (125ml) cream
1	teaspoon chopped fresh thyme

LIGHTLY grease a 20cm x 20cm baking dish. With the skins on, steam the potatoes whole until well cooked. Peel cooked potatoes and mash together with the Philly, flour, egg, herbs, salt and pepper.

ROLL the potato mixture into 1cm tubes and cut each into 2cm lengths (lightly roll in extra flour if sticky). Gently flatten each piece of gnocchi with a fork.

BRING a large saucepan of salted water to the boil. Drop the gnocchi (about 12 at a time) into the saucepan. When they float to the top, cook for a further 30 seconds. Remove from saucepan with a slotted spoon and place in the prepared baking dish.

SPOON the mushrooms, prosciutto, cream and thyme over the gnocchi. Place under a hot grill for 20 minutes or until topping is bubbling and golden.

SCALLOP RISOTTO

PREPARATION TIME: 5 MINUTES
COOKING TIME: 25 MINUTES
SERVES: 2

1	tablespoon olive oil
1	medium leek, sliced
1	clove garlic, crushed
1 1/2	cups (300g) arborio rice
3/4	cup (185ml) dry white wine
4	cups (1 litre) chicken stock, boiling
150g	(1 cup) shelled fresh peas
12	medium (250g) scallops
1	teaspoon grated lemon rind
125g	block PHILADELPHIA Cream Cheese, softened
	salt and pepper, to taste

HEAT the oil in large saucepan and cook the leek and garlic over medium heat for 5 minutes, or until leek is soft. Stir in the rice until translucent and well coated with oil.

ADD the white wine and cook stirring until the liquid is absorbed. Gradually add the hot stock in small quantities, stirring until most of the stock is absorbed before adding more.

ADD peas, scallops and lemon rind to the pan. Cover and cook for 5 minutes, or until scallops are tender. Gently stir through Philly until melted and combined. Season to taste and serve immediately.

PHILLY GNOCCHI

SCALLOP RISOTTO

FISH IN A PHILLY CHILLI CRUST

FISH IN A LEMON GARLIC JACKET

FISH IN A PHILLY CHILLI CRUST

PREPARATION TIME: 15 MINUTES
COOKING TIME: 30 MINUTES
SERVES 4

1	750g snapper or 8 whole garfish
125g	block PHILADELPHIA Cream Cheese, softened
1/4	cup (60ml) sweet chilli sauce
3	spring onions, chopped
1	tablespoon finely chopped parsley or coriander
	sweet chilli sauce, for serving
	spring onions, chopped, for serving

CLEAN fish and pat dry with paper towel. Blend Philly, chilli sauce, spring onions and herbs until smooth. Spread over both sides of the fish.

PLACE fish on a baking tray lined with baking paper. Bake at 180°C for 30 minutes for snapper or 10 minutes for garfish, or until fish flakes easily with a fork.

SERVE garnished with extra chilli sauce and spring onion.

KRAFT KITCHENS HANDY HINTS

SUBSTITUTE any fresh fish for snapper or garfish – adjust the cooking time accordingly.

FISH IN A LEMON GARLIC JACKET

PREPARATION TIME: 15 MINUTES
COOKING TIME: 30 MINUTES
SERVES: 4

1	750g snapper or 8 whole garfish
125g	block PHILADELPHIA Cream Cheese, softened
	rind and juice of 1 lemon
1	clove garlic, finely chopped
1/3	cup parsley
2/3	cup (50g) fresh ciabatta breadcrumbs

CLEAN fish and pat dry with paper towel. Mix Philly with 1/2 of the combined lemon rind, juice, garlic, parsley and breadcrumbs to form a paste.

SPREAD over both sides of the fish. Pat the remainder of the crumb mix onto the Philly paste, seasoning to taste with salt and pepper.

PLACE on a baking tray lined with baking paper and bake at 180°C for 30 minutes for snapper or 10 minutes for garfish, until fish is cooked through.

KRAFT KITCHENS HANDY HINTS

SUBSTITUTE any fresh fish for snapper or garfish – adjust the cooking time accordingly.

BAKED LAMB LOIN WITH PHILADELPHIA

BLUESTONE, MELBOURNE, VICTORIA

PREPARATION TIME: 15 MINUTES
COOKING TIME: 20 MINUTES
SERVES: 4

4	160g lamb straps, boneless loins, or fillets
2	teaspoons olive oil
250g	block PHILADELPHIA Cream Cheese, softened
1/4	cup finely chopped oregano or marjoram
	salt and pepper, to taste
8	sheets filo pastry
75g	butter, melted
	apricot chutney, to serve

SEASON the lamb loin with salt and pepper. Heat the olive oil in a frying pan and cook the seasoned lamb over high heat for about 3 minutes each side, or until well browned. Remove from heat and set aside to cool slightly.

COMBINE the softened Philly, oregano, salt and pepper and blend until smooth. Spread the Philly mixture evenly over each lamb loin.

BRUSH the filo pastry sheets with butter and assemble into 4 pairs. Place one lamb loin along the short edge of each pastry bundle. Fold in the sides, then roll up to firmly enclose the lamb and form a parcel. Brush with remaining butter.

PLACE the lamb parcels seam-side down on a non-stick baking tray. Bake at 180°C for 15–20 minutes, or until the pastry is crisp and golden. Serve with apricot chutney.

BAKED LAMB LOIN WITH PHILADELPHIA

RUBBED KANGAROO AND PHILLY SALAD

RUBBED KANGAROO
AND PHILLY SALAD

PREPARATION TIME: 30 MINUTES
COOKING TIME: 30 MINUTES
SERVES: 4

250g   block PHILADELPHIA Cream Cheese
1/4   cup olive oil
1   clove garlic, crushed
1   medium (300g) sweet potato, peeled and thinly sliced
    butter and garlic spray
4   150g kangaroo sirloin fillets or lamb backstraps
2   teaspoons dried native mint
200g   lettuce mix
1   yellow capsicum, thinly sliced

HONEY BALSAMIC DRESSING

1 1/2   tablespoons balsamic vinegar
3   teaspoons honey
1   teaspoon mountain pepper

PLACE the whole Philly block on a baking tray, drizzle with oil and top with garlic. Bake at 180°C for 25–30 minutes, or until lightly golden. Remove and cut the Philly into 16 pieces and retain the oil in the pan for the dressing. Arrange the sweet potato slices in a single layer on a baking tray lined with baking paper. Spray well with butter and garlic spray. Bake at 180°C for about 20–30 minutes or until crisp and golden.

RUB the kangaroo fillet with the native mint. Preheat a chargrill or barbecue pan until hot. Add the meat and cook for 5–10 minutes, or to required taste. Remove from heat, loosely cover with foil and let stand 2–3 minutes. Cut fillets into thin slices on the diagonal.

ARRANGE the lettuce mix on serving plates. Top with baked Philly pieces, sweet potato, kangaroo and capsicum.

HONEY BALSAMIC DRESSING

COMBINE the reserved oil, balsamic vinegar, honey and mountain pepper. Drizzle with dressing and serve immediately.

SHITAKE BEEF WITH PHILLY PEPPERCORN MASH

PREPARATION TIME: 30 MINUTES
COOKING TIME: 20–30 MINUTES
SERVES: 4

2	large (600g) potatoes, peeled and chopped
125g	block PHILADELPHIA Cream Cheese, softened
1/4	cup (60ml) milk
	salt and pepper
1 1/2	tablespoons green peppercorns in brine, rinsed
1	tablespoon olive oil
30g	butter, melted
4	200g beef fillet steaks
150g	golden shallots, peeled and thickly sliced
100g	shitake mushrooms, halved
1	cup (250ml) chicken stock
1/2	cup (125ml) port
1-2	teaspoons cornflour, blended with
	1 tablespoon cold water

BOIL, steam or microwave potatoes until tender. Drain and mash with Philly, milk, salt and pepper until smooth. Fold in peppercorns, cover and keep warm.

HEAT half of the combined oil and butter in a heavy based frying pan. Cook steaks over medium heat until cooked as desired. Loosely wrap in foil to allow meat to rest. Heat the remaining oil and butter in pan and cook shallots over a gentle heat until softened. Stir in the mushrooms, stock and port; simmer until the sauce is reduced by one-third. Thicken with the cornflour mixture if desired.

SPOON a dollop of potato mash onto each serving plate, top with steaks and drizzle with the mushroom sauce. Serve immediately.

PUMPKIN, CAULIFLOWER AND CHICKPEA CURRY

PREPARATION TIME: 15 MINUTES
COOKING TIME: 25 MINUTES
SERVES: 4

2	tablespoons oil
1	large brown onion, cut into thin wedges
1/4	cup korma curry paste
1kg	butternut pumpkin, cut into 2 1/2 cm cubes
1/4	medium cauliflower, cut into florets
2	large (600g) desiree potatoes, cut into 2 1/2 cm cubes
410g	can chopped peeled tomatoes
225g	can chickpeas, drained
1 1/2	cups (375ml) vegetable or chicken stock
2	tablespoons desiccated coconut
125g	block PHILADELPHIA Cream Cheese, softened
1	bunch (60g) coriander leaves, roughly chopped
1-2	teaspoons lemon juice, to taste
	salt and pepper

HEAT the oil in a large saucepan. Add the onion and cook gently for 5 minutes, or until it is soft and lightly browned. Add the curry paste and cook a further 1 minute, until fragrant.

ADD the vegetables, tomatoes, chickpeas, stock and coconut. Bring mixture to the boil. Simmer, covered over low heat for approximately 15 minutes, or until vegetables are just tender. Gently stir through the Philly until blended. Add coriander, lemon juice, salt and pepper. Serve on a bed of steamed rice.

SHITAKE BEEF WITH PHILLY
PEPPERCORN MASH

PUMPKIN, CAULIFLOWER
AND CHICKPEA CURRY

GARLIC CHICKEN

PREPARATION TIME: 25 MINUTES
COOKING TIME: 1.25 HOURS
SERVES: 6

1	large bunch (60g) continental or curly parsley, chopped
1/4	cup (60ml) oil
1.8kg	free-range chicken, neck removed
125g	block PHILADELPHIA Cream Cheese, softened
	salt and pepper, to taste
1	cup (80g) fresh white breadcrumbs
1	small red onion, finely chopped
1	egg
400g	frozen peas
2	heads of garlic, cloves separated, unpeeled
2	tablespoons olive oil
1	teaspoon finely chopped thyme

COMBINE parsley and oil in a food processor and process until smooth.

WASH and clean the cavity of the chicken. Pat dry inside and out using paper towel.

COMBINE the Philly, parsley mixture, salt and pepper in a bowl. Gently loosen the skin of the chicken away from the breast. Place half of the mixture under the skin. Add breadcrumbs, onion and egg to the remaining Philly mixture to form a stuffing. Use this to stuff the cavity of the chicken.

PLACE the chicken in a large casserole dish with the peas. Arrange the unpeeled garlic cloves around the chicken. Drizzle with olive oil and sprinkle with thyme. Cover tightly with foil or a lid.

BAKE at 160°C for 1 hour. Remove the foil and bake for a further 15 minutes until golden brown and cooked through. Serve with roasted garlic cloves.

GARLIC CHICKEN

DATE AND GINGER
PORK MEATBALLS

PREPARATION: 10 MINUTES
COOKING TIME: 10 MINUTES
SERVES: 4

750g   pork mince
125g   PHILADELPHIA Spreadable Cream Cheese
1   medium red onion, finely chopped
1   cup (185g) dates, pitted and halved
1/4   cup finely chopped coriander
1   tablespoon finely grated ginger
2   tablespoons vegetable oil
    cous cous, to serve

SAUCE

1   medium onion, grated
2   teaspoons finely grated ginger
    salt and pepper, to taste
1/2   teaspoon turmeric
1/4   teaspoon cumin
1   teaspoon paprika
1/4   cup roughly chopped coriander
1/4   cup roughly chopped parsley
1 1/2   cups (375ml) water
    juice of 1 lemon

COMBINE the pork, Philly, onion, dates, coriander and ginger in a large bowl. Chill for 15 minutes until firm, then roll into walnut-sized balls.

HEAT the oil in a large frying pan over medium heat. Cook meatballs in batches until well browned.

ADD all the sauce ingredients to the pan except for the lemon juice. Bring to the boil, add meatballs, reduce heat and simmer for 20 minutes or until reduced by half. Add the lemon juice and stir through. Serve with cous cous.

DATE AND GINGER
PORK MEATBALLS

VEAL STUFFED WITH CAPSICUM, PHILLY AND BASIL

PREPARATION TIME: 15 MINUTES
COOKING TIME: 25 MINUTES
SERVES: 4

125g   block PHILADELPHIA Cream Cheese, softened
 60g   KRAFT Blue Cheese or goat's cheese
         salt and pepper, to taste
    4   100g veal steaks
    1   bunch (60g) basil leaves
    2   large yellow capsicum, seeded and sliced
 50g   spinach leaves
    1   tablespoon (20g) butter
    1   tablespoon olive oil

SAUCE

 30g   butter
    2   cloves garlic, crushed
400g   can peeled tomatoes, blended
  1/4 cup (60ml) dry white wine
  1/4 cup (60ml) water
    1   tablespoon (25g) tomato paste
    1   teaspoon sugar, to taste
         salt and pepper, to taste

COMBINE the Philly, Blue Cheese, salt, and pepper in a small bowl and blend until smooth.

COVER the veal steaks with plastic wrap. Using a rolling pin or mallet, flatten the veal to 1cm thickness. Spread the cheese mixture over the flattened veal steaks, leaving 2cm uncovered along one edge. Top the cheese mixture with basil leaves, capsicum and spinach.

ROLL the veal tightly towards the uncovered edge to enclose the filling. Secure with toothpicks.

HEAT butter and olive oil in a heavy-based ovenproof pan. Cook the veal over medium-high heat, about 3 minutes or until well browned. Transfer the pan to the oven and bake at 180°C for 15–20 minutes or until the veal is tender. Serve hot with sauce.

SAUCE

HEAT the butter in a medium-sized frying pan. Sautée garlic, stirring for 1 minute. Add tomato, wine, water and tomato paste. Bring the mixture to the boil, then simmer uncovered, over low heat for about 15 minutes – until sauce is slightly thickened. Season with sugar, salt and pepper.

VEAL STUFFED WITH
CAPSICUM, PHILLY AND BASIL

dessert

BLUEBERRY CROISSANT PUDDING

PREPARATION TIME: 15 MINUTES
COOKING TIME: 40 MINUTES
SERVES: 4–6

butter for greasing
3 large croissants, cut lengthwise into thick slices
1 punnet (150g) blueberries
250g block PHILADELPHIA Cream Cheese, softened
2/3 cup (150g) caster sugar
1 cup (250ml) cream
1 cup (250ml) milk
2 eggs
1 teaspoon vanilla extract
1/4 cup (45g) brown sugar, lightly packed

GREASE a 6 cup (1.5 litre) capacity ovenproof dish. Arrange the croissant slices in a single overlapping layer in the base of the baking dish. Sprinkle with blueberries.

BEAT the Philly and sugar until smooth. Gradually pour in the cream, milk, eggs and vanilla until mixed. Pour the mixture over the croissants and leave to stand for 30 minutes.

SPRINKLE the pudding with brown sugar. Bake at 180°C in a waterbath for 40 minutes, or until set and golden. Serve hot with cream or ice-cream.

BLUEBERRY CROISSANT PUDDING

VANILLA AND VODKA CHEESECAKE MOUSSE

PREPARATION TIME: 20 MINUTES
REFRIGERATION TIME: 2–3 HOURS
COOKING TIME: 3–5 MINUTES
SERVES: 8–10

1 vanilla bean pod or 2 teaspoons vanilla essence
1/4 cup (55g) caster sugar, for syrup
1/4 cup (60ml) vodka
2 250g blocks PHILADELPHIA Cream Cheese, softened
1/2 cup (110g) caster sugar, for batter
3 teaspoons gelatine, dissolved in
1/4 cup (60ml) boiling water
1 1/2 cups (375ml) cream, lightly whipped

LINE a 20cm springform pan with baking paper.

SPLIT the vanilla bean lengthwise and scrape out the seeds with a knife. Combine the bean pod, seeds, sugar and the vodka in a small saucepan. Stir over low heat until all the sugar is dissolved. Bring the mixture to the boil, then simmer for 1 minute. Cool, and discard the vanilla bean pod.

BEAT the Philly and extra sugar in a large bowl with an electric mixer, until smooth. Add the vodka syrup and gelatine mixture; mix well. Gently fold the whipped cream into the mixture until combined.

POUR into the prepared pan. Refrigerate for 2–3 hours, or until set.

PEAR AND VANILLA CHEESECAKE

PREPARATION TIME: 25 MINUTES
COOKING TIME: 65 MINUTES
SERVES: 10–12

1 1/4 cups (155g) 'Gingernut' biscuit crumbs
60g butter, melted
3 250g blocks PHILADELPHIA Cream Cheese, softened
1 cup (225g) caster sugar
1 1/2 tablespoons custard powder
1 cup (250ml) cream
3 eggs, lightly beaten
seeds of 1 vanilla bean
410g can pear halves, well drained
1/3 cup (60g) brown sugar, lightly packed

COMBINE the biscuit crumbs and butter. Press mixture into the base of a 24cm springform pan, lined with baking paper. Refrigerate.

BEAT the Philly and sugar in a large bowl with an electric mixer until just combined. Mix the custard powder and 1/4 cup cream in a small bowl until smooth.

COMBINE with the remaining cream, eggs and vanilla seeds. Gradually beat into the Philly mixture until smooth.

POUR the mixture into the prepared crumb crust, and bake at 150°C for 1 hour or until just set. Allow to cool in the oven, with the door ajar.

TOP the cheesecake with pear halves and sprinkle with brown sugar. Place under a hot grill until the sugar is melted and the pears are cooked. Refrigerate for 30 minutes before serving.

VANILLA AND VODKA CHEESECAKE MOUSSE

PEAR AND VANILLA CHEESECAKE

BALSAMIC STRAWBERRY CHEESECAKE

PREPARATION TIME: 30 MINUTES PLUS
OVERNIGHT REFRIGERATION
COOKING TIME: 60 MINUTES
SERVES: 12–14

1/3 cup (80ml) balsamic vinegar

1/2 cup (125g) caster sugar

2 punnets (500g) strawberries, halved

1 1/4 cups (185g) sweet biscuit crumbs

90g butter, melted

3 250g blocks PHILADELPHIA Cream Cheese, softened

1 1/3 cups (300g) caster sugar, extra

1 cup (250ml) sour cream

3 eggs

COMBINE the balsamic vinegar and sugar in a large bowl. Stir until the sugar is mostly dissolved. Add the strawberries, stirring to coat. Stand for at least one hour, then drain the strawberries and reserve the syrup.

LINE the base and sides of a 24cm springform pan with baking paper. Wrap the outside of the pan with two layers of foil and secure with string. Combine the biscuit crumbs and butter in a small bowl. Press the crumb mixture into the base of the lined, prepared pan. Chill until firm.

BEAT the Philly and extra sugar with an electric mixer until just combined. Add the sour cream. Beat until smooth. Gradually add eggs and beat until just combined.

ARRANGE half of the halved strawberries over the prepared biscuit base. Pour the Philly mixture over them and place the springform pan in a large baking dish.

FILL the dish with enough boiling water to come halfway up the sides of the pan.

BAKE at 160°C for 30–35 minutes, then lightly cover with a sheet of foil to prevent over-browning. Bake for a further 15 minutes, or until cheesecake is just set. Cool in the oven for 1 hour with the door ajar. Chill overnight.

PLACE the reserved syrup in a small saucepan and bring to the boil. Simmer over medium heat for 5 minutes, or until mixture is syrupy and reduced to 1/2 cup. Allow the syrup to cool before spooning it over the set cheesecake and topping with remaining strawberries.

PINEAPPLE CHEESECAKE

PINEAPPLE CHEESECAKE

DISTORTA, COLLINGWOOD, VICTORIA

PREPARATION TIME: 20 MINUTES
COOKING TIME: 10 MINUTES
SERVES: 10–12

1 1/4	cups (155g) sweet biscuit crumbs
80g	butter, melted
2/3	cup (150g) caster sugar
1/2	cup (125ml) water
3	eggs
1	tablespoon gelatine, dissolved in 1/4 cup (60ml) boiling water, cooled
2	250g block PHILADELPHIA Cream Cheese, softened
450g	can crushed pineapple in syrup, well drained
300ml	(1 1/3 cups) thickened cream, lightly whipped
	seasonal fresh fruit to decorate

COMBINE the biscuit crumbs and butter. Press the mixture into the base of a 24cm springform pan, lined with baking paper. Refrigerate.

COMBINE sugar and water in medium pan. Stir over medium heat until sugar is dissolved. Bring to the boil and keep at a rolling boil for 6 minutes, or until mixture reaches softball stage – or 118°C on a candy thermometer. Meanwhile beat eggs in a large bowl with an electric mixer until light and creamy. Gradually pour in the hot sugar syrup and combine. Add gelatine mixture and continue to beat a further 3–4 minutes until mixture is pale, thick and lukewarm.

BEAT Philly in a large bowl with an electric mixer until smooth. Fold in the egg mixture, crushed pineapple and whipped cream. Pour into the prepared pan and refrigerate until set. Decorate with fresh fruit.

KRAFT KITCHENS HANDY HINTS

DON'T be tempted to substitute canned pineapple for fresh in this recipe filling. The enzymes in fresh pineapple will prevent the gelatine from setting the cheesecake.

APRICOT CRUMBLE CHEESECAKE

PREPARATION TIME: 20 MINUTES
REFRIGERATION TIME: 2 HOURS
SERVES: 10

2	cups 'Butternut Snap' biscuit crumbs (2 packets)
70g	butter, melted
1/4	cup (50g) hazelnuts, toasted, finely chopped
2	tablespoons desiccated coconut
1	teaspoon cinnamon
1/2	teaspoon nutmeg
2	250g blocks PHILADELPHIA Cream Cheese, softened
3/4	cup (165g) caster sugar
1	tablespoon gelatine dissolved in
1/4	cup (60ml) boiling water, cooled
2	tablespoons lemon juice
1	cup (250ml) cream, lightly whipped
425g	can apricots in natural syrup, chopped

COMBINE the biscuit crumbs, butter, chopped hazelnuts, coconut and spices. Divide the crumb mixture in half, pressing half into the base of a 20cm springform pan lined with baking paper. Chill until firm.

BEAT the Philly and sugar with an electric mixer until smooth. Beat in the gelatine mixture and lemon juice until blended. Fold in the whipped cream. Pour the mixture into the prepared pan. Swirl the apricots through the mixture.

TOP the cheesecake with the remaining crumb mixture. Chill for 2 hours or until set.

SUMMER CHARLOTTE

PREPARATION TIME: 20 MINUTES
REFRIGERATION TIME: 1–2 HOURS
SERVES: 6–8

20–25	small sponge finger biscuits (Savoiardi)
425g	can mixed berries, drained and juice reserved
1	cup (250ml) blackcurrant juice
2	tablespoons caster sugar
250g	block PHILADELPHIA Cream Cheese, softened
1	tablespoon caster sugar, extra
1/2	cup (125ml) cream
1	teaspoon gelatine, dissolved in 1 tablespoon boiling water, cooled
125g	strawberries, hulled and chopped
	fresh raspberries, to serve
	raspberry sauce, to serve

LINE a 16cm x 22cm loaf pan with plastic wrap. Trim the finger biscuits to line base and sides of pan, leaving aside some biscuits for the top.

COMBINE the reserved berry juice, blackcurrant juice and caster sugar in a saucepan over moderate heat until dissolved. Bring to the boil, reduce heat and simmer until reduced by half, about 5–10 minutes. Cool. Reserve 1/2 cup of the juice mixture and brush remainder over the biscuits in the loaf pan.

BEAT the Philly and sugar in a bowl with an electric mixer until smooth. Add in the cream and dissolved gelatine and mix until thick. Fold in the mixed berries and strawberries. Pour the mixture into the prepared pan. Top with reserved biscuits and brush with the remaining reserved juice. Chill for 1–2 hours or until set. Invert onto a serving plate and serve sliced with fresh raspberries and raspberry sauce, if desired.

KRAFT KITCHENS HANDY HINTS

FOR an easy raspberry sauce: process 150g frozen or fresh raspberries in the food processor until smooth. Push the fruit through a fine sieve into a bowl. Sweeten sauce with 1–2 tablespoons icing sugar and serve.

APRICOT CRUMBLE CHEESECAKE

SUMMER CHARLOTTE

ALMOND GINGER
CREAM MERINGUE

PREPARATION TIME: 30 MINUTES
COOKING TIME: 1 HOUR
MAKES: 10

4	egg whites
1	cup (225g) caster sugar
1/3	cup (125g) almond meal, toasted
1/3	cup (80g) flaked almonds, toasted
250g	block PHILADELPHIA Cream Cheese, softened
1	tablespoon honey
125g	glace ginger, finely chopped

LINE two baking trays with baking paper and trace
10 x 7cm diameter circles on each sheet.

BEAT the egg whites until stiff. Add the caster
sugar, one tablespoon at a time, and beat until the
sugar is dissolved. Fold in the almond meal.

SPOON two tablespoons of meringue onto each
circle and lightly spread to the edges of the circle.
Top with flaked almonds. Bake at 140°C for one
hour, then cool in the oven with the door ajar.

MIX Philly, honey and ginger until combined.
Sandwich two meringues together with the Philly
mixture. Serve immediately.

KRAFT KITCHENS HANDY HINTS

MADE in miniature, these delicious meringues make
wonderful dinner party petits fours.

ALMOND GINGER CREAM MERINGUE

MOROCCAN DELIGHT

PREPARATION TIME: 20 MINUTES
COOKING TIME: 10 MINUTES
MAKES: 16

2 tablespoons caster sugar

2 tablespoons water

1/3 cup (25g) finely chopped Turkish apricots

2 tablespoons finely chopped shelled pistachio nuts

250g block PHILADELPHIA Cream Cheese

1 tablespoon rose water

COMBINE the sugar and water in a saucepan over low heat, stirring constantly until the sugar has dissolved. Allow to cool. Stir through the chopped apricots and pistachios. Cut the Philly into 16 cubes. Roll the Philly cubes in the apricot mixture, pressing firmly to coat.

PLACE the cubes on a baking tray lined with baking paper and bake at 180°C for 10 minutes or until golden. Drizzle with rose water and serve.

LIME AND GINGER PHILLY BITES

PREPARATION TIME: 20 MINUTES
COOKING TIME: 10 MINUTES
MAKES: 16

250g block PHILADELPHIA Cream Cheese

1/3 cup ginger and lime marmalade

1 teaspoon freshly grated ginger
almond bread to serve

CUT the Philly into 16 cubes and place on a baking tray lined with baking paper.

COMBINE the marmalade and ginger and heat in a microwave-safe bowl on high for 15 seconds. Stir until smooth and slightly runny. Drizzle the Philly with marmalade until coated.

BAKE at 180°C for 10 minutes or until jam is bubbly. Serve warm or cold with almond bread.

LAMINGTON PHILLY BITES

PREPARATION TIME: 20 MINUTES
COOKING TIME: 10 MINUTES
MAKES: 24

250g block PHILADELPHIA Cream Cheese, softened

1 tablespoon strawberry jam

1/3 cup (125ml) mint flavoured chocolate topping

2 cups chocolate cake crumbs

1 cup (60g) shredded coconut.

MIX Philly and jam thoroughly in a small bowl. Cover and refrigerate for 20 minutes or until firm. Using damp hands, roll teaspoons of Philly mixture into balls.

DIP the balls into chocolate topping, roll in chocolate cake crumbs and then toss in shredded coconut.

BAKE at 180°C for 10 minutes or until the coconut is golden. Serve warm or cold.

KRAFT KITCHENS HANDY HINT

DO not be tempted to combine the cake crumbs and coconut for ease; the results are not as good.

MOROCCAN DELIGHT
LIME AND GINGER PHILLY BITES
LAMINGTON PHILLY BITES

RASPBERRY RIPPLE ICE-CREAM

PREPARATION TIME: 20 MINUTES
COOKING TIME: 6–8 MINUTES
SERVES: 4

2	250g blocks PHILADELPHIA Cream Cheese, softened
1/2	cup (110g) caster sugar
1	cup (250ml) cream
1	teaspoon vanilla
4	eggs, separated
300g	packet frozen raspberries, thawed
1/3	cup light corn syrup

BEAT the Philly and sugar with an electric mixer until smooth. Add the cream, vanilla and egg yolks. Beat until smooth and slightly thickened.

BEAT the egg whites in a clean, dry bowl until stiff peaks form and gently fold into the Philly mixture. Pour the ice-cream into a shallow metal container and allow to semi-freeze.

PUREE the berries. Sieve to remove all seeds. Combine the berry puree and corn syrup in a small saucepan and stir over medium heat until the mixture thickens and reduces by half. Cool.

SPOON the berry mixture over the semi-set ice-cream and gently swirl through. Freeze until firm.

RASPBERRY RIPPLE ICE-CREAM

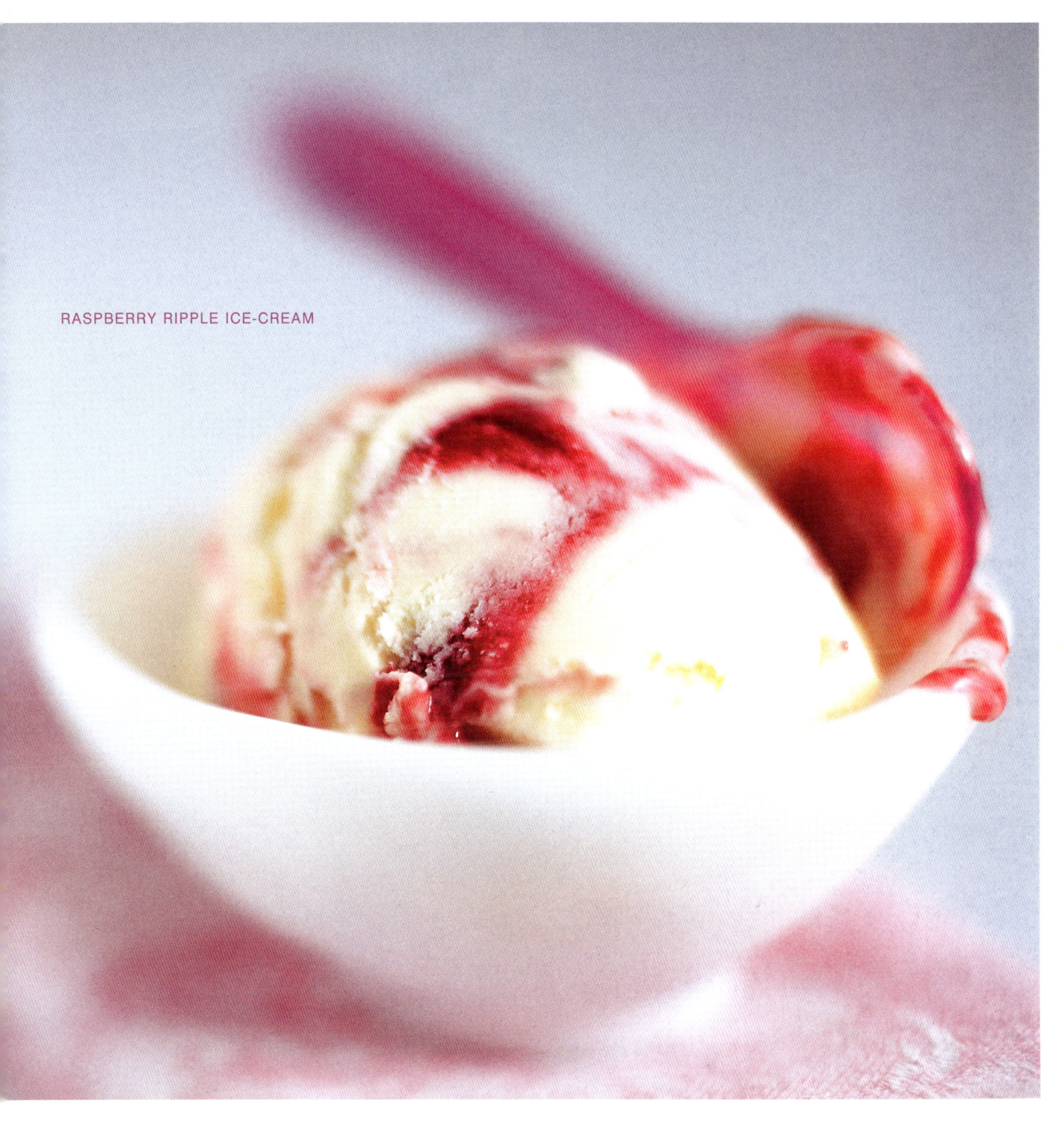

WHITE TOBLERONE AND PISTACHIO ICE-CREAM

PREPARATION TIME: 20 MINUTES
REFRIGERATION TIME: 2 HOURS
SERVES: 4

2	250g blocks PHILADELPHIA Cream Cheese, softened
1/4	cup (55g) caster sugar
1	teaspoon grated orange rind
1	teaspoon vanilla essence
4	eggs, separated
200g	white Toblerone, melted and cooled
1/2	cup (75g) shelled pistachio nuts, chopped

BEAT the Philly, sugar, orange rind and vanilla essence with an electric mixer until smooth. Add egg yolks and beat until slightly thickened. Stir in the melted chocolate until combined.

BEAT the egg whites in a clean, dry bowl until stiff peaks form and gently fold into the Philly mixture. Pour the ice-cream into a shallow metal container and allow to semi-freeze before folding through the nuts. Freeze until firm.

WHITE TOBLERONE AND PISTACHIO ICE-CREAM

BAILEY'S ICE-CREAM

PREPARATION TIME: 20 MINUTES
REFRIGERATION TIME: 2 HOURS
SERVES: 4

2	250g blocks PHILADELPHIA Cream Cheese, softened
1/2	cup (110g) caster sugar
1	teaspoon vanilla essence
1	cup (250ml) cream
4	eggs, separated
2/3	cup (165ml) Bailey's liqueur

BEAT the Philly, sugar and vanilla essence until smooth. Add the cream, egg yolks and liqueur. Beat until the mixture has slightly thickened.

BEAT the egg whites in a clean, dry bowl until stiff peaks form and gently fold them into the Philly mixture. Pour the ice-cream into a shallow metal container. Freeze until firm.

KRAFT KITCHENS HANDY HINTS

FOR that extra special touch: add a shot of Bailey's liqueur to the ice-cream once served.

BAILEY'S ICE-CREAM

PHILADELPHIA PANNACOTTA
WITH CITRUS SAUCE

CATALINA, ROSE BAY, NEW SOUTH WALES

PREPARATION TIME: 30 MINUTES
REFRIGERATION TIME: 3–4 HOURS
SERVES: 4

   1   cup (250ml) cream
 1/4   cup (55g) caster sugar
   1   tablespoon brandy
   1   vanilla bean pod, split and seeds removed
250g   block PHILADELPHIA Cream Cheese, softened
   1   teaspoon gelatine, dissolved in
       1 tablespoon boiling water, cooled
   2   egg whites
       citrus rind strips, extra, to garnish

CITRUS SAUCE

 1/3   cup (90ml) water
 1/2   cup (110g) caster sugar
       rind of 1 lemon
       rind of 1 orange
       rind of 1 lime

COMBINE the cream, sugar, brandy, vanilla pod and seeds in a saucepan to just below boiling point. Remove from the heat and discard the vanilla pod.

BEAT the Philly in a bowl until smooth. Gradually beat in the infused cream and dissolved gelatine until combined.

IN a clean bowl, beat the egg whites until stiff peaks form. Gently fold the egg whites into the Philly mixture, and pour into 4 x 1/2 cup (125ml) capacity moulds. Refrigerate for 3–4 hours or until set.

INVERT the pannacotta onto serving plates, drizzle with citrus sauce and top with the citrus rind.

CITRUS SAUCE

PLACE water, sugar and half the rind in a small saucepan. Stir over low heat until the sugar is dissolved. Bring the mixture to the boil, and simmer about 5 minutes, or until it is slightly syrupy and reduced. Strain and refrigerate until cool.

PHILADELPHIA PANNACOTTA
WITH CITRUS SAUCE

QUINCE AND PISTACHIO TURNOVERS

RICKY RICARDO'S, NOOSA HEADS, QUEENSLAND

PREPARATION TIME: 1 HOUR
COOKING TIME: 3 HOURS
SERVES: 6

2 large quinces
1 1/2 cups (375ml) water
3/4 cup (165g) caster sugar
juice of 1/2 lemon
1 clove
1/2 cinnamon stick
1 cup (125g) plain flour
125g block PHILADELPHIA Cream Cheese, cut into cubes
75g unsalted butter, chilled and chopped
1 cup (250ml) milk
3 egg yolks
1/3 cup (75g) caster sugar
1/4 cup (25g) cornflour
1/4 cup (35g) shelled pistachio nuts, chopped
1 egg, combined with 2 tablespoons milk

PEEL, quarter and core the quinces. Reserve the peelings, cores and seeds, and tie together in a muslin bag. Place the quinces, bag, water, sugar, lemon juice and spices in a heavy-based saucepan with a tight-fitting lid. Gently simmer for 2–3 hours, or until quinces are tender and bright pink. Carefully remove quinces from the syrup and transfer to a tray; cover and refrigerate. Boil the cooking liquid a further 10 minutes or until syrup is slightly thick; strain.

COMBINE the flour, Philly and butter in a food processor and process until dough just comes together. Knead lightly and cover with plastic wrap. Refrigerate for one hour or until firm.

HEAT the milk just to the boiling point, then remove from heat. In a medium-sized bowl, beat the egg yolks, sugar and cornflour with an electric mixer until thick. Pour the hot milk – a little at a time – into the mixture, beating until smooth.

RETURN the mixture to the saucepan and stir over medium heat until thick; do not boil. Cool covered with plastic wrap pressed onto the cream, to stop a skin from forming across the top.

TO assemble, cut the pastry into 12 equal pieces. Shape into balls and roll each ball out with a rolling pin into 10cm circles, dusting with flour to avoid sticking. Place one tablespoon of pastry cream on the front half of each circle, sprinkle with chopped pistachios and top with pieces of quince. Fold the pastry over and seal with eggwash. Place all the turnovers on a baking tray. Bake at 180°C for 20 minutes or until golden.

SERVE, placing two turnovers on each plate; drizzled with reduced quince syrup and scattered with pistachios.

QUINCE AND PISTACHIO TURNOVERS

PEACH CHEESECAKE MUFFINS

PREPARATION TIME: 20 MINUTES
COOKING TIME: 25 MINUTES
MAKES: 12

2   250g block PHILADELPHIA Cream Cheese, softened
1   cup (225g) caster sugar
2   eggs
150g   ground almonds
1/2   cup (125ml) sour cream
2   tablespoons custard powder
2   medium peaches, sliced, or 1/2 x 440g can
2   tablespoons maple syrup

LINE the bases of a 12 x 1/2 cup (125ml) capacity muffin pan.

BEAT the Philly and sugar in a medium bowl until just combined. Add the eggs, ground almonds, sour cream and custard powder, beating until smooth. Spoon into the prepared pan. Top the mixture with peach slices, and drizzle with maple syrup.

BAKE at 180°C for 20–25 minutes or until set and golden.

COCONUT AND LIME TEACAKE

PREPARATION TIME: 30 MINUTES
COOKING TIME: 1 1/4 HOURS
SERVES: 8

250g   block PHILADELPHIA Cream Cheese, softened
1   cup (185g) grated palm sugar or brown sugar, lightly packed
    grated rind and juice of 2 limes
2   eggs, separated
1   cup (125g) self-raising flour, sifted
1   cup (250ml) coconut milk
1 1/2   cups (90g) shredded coconut
1/2   cup (45g) shredded or flaked coconut, extra

SYRUP

1   cup (250ml) water
1   cup (250g) sugar
    grated rind and juice of 1 lime
    cinnamon stick
10   cardamom pods, squashed with the back of a cook's knife
2   star anise

GREASE and line a 20cm square cake pan with baking paper.

BEAT the Philly and sugar with an electric beater until smooth. Add the lime rind, juice and egg yolks. Stir in the sifted flour, coconut milk and shredded coconut in two batches until combined.

IN a small bowl, beat egg whites until stiff peaks form. Gently fold egg whites into Philly mixture until combined.

POUR the mixture into the lined pan. Sprinkle with extra coconut and bake at 170°C for 1 1/4 hours, or until set and golden. Pour the hot syrup over the hot cake. Stand for 10 minutes, or until syrup is absorbed into cake before serving.

SYRUP

COMBINE all ingredients in a small pan. Bring mixture to the boil, and simmer over low heat for 20 minutes until thick and syrupy. Strain.

PEACH CHEESECAKE MUFFINS

COCONUT AND LIME TEACAKE

LIME AND PHILLY PUDDING WITH ORANGE CARAMEL SAUCE

HUGO'S, BONDI BEACH, NEW SOUTH WALES

PREPARATION TIME: 20 MINUTES
COOKING TIME: 30–35 MINUTES
SERVES: 6

	butter and caster sugar, for greasing and dusting
250g	block PHILADELPHIA Cream Cheese, softened
4	eggs, separated
	grated rind of 1 lime
2	teaspoons lime juice
2	teaspoons vanilla essence
2	teaspoons custard powder
1/2	cup (110g) caster sugar

ORANGE CARAMEL SAUCE

1	cup (225g) caster sugar
1/2	cup (125ml) water
1	cup (250ml) orange juice
1	cinnamon stick
2	cloves

GREASE 6 x 2/3 cup (165ml) capacity ovenproof dishes and dust with sugar.

BEAT the Philly in a large bowl with an electric mixer until smooth. Add the egg yolks, one at a time, beating until the mixture is thick and creamy. Add the rind, juice, vanilla and custard powder. Beat until the mixture is smooth and thick.

IN a large, clean bowl, beat egg whites until soft peaks form. Add the caster sugar, one tablespoon at a time, and beat until mixture is thick and the sugar has dissolved.

WITH a large metal spoon, gently fold the egg white mixture into the Philly mixture until combined. Spoon into the prepared moulds. Place moulds in a large baking dish. Fill the dish with enough boiling water to come halfway up the sides of the moulds. Bake at 160°C for 30–35 minutes, or until the puddings have risen and appear golden. Do not open oven door during cooking. Serve immediately drizzled with Orange Caramel Sauce.

ORANGE CARAMEL SAUCE

COMBINE caster sugar and water in a medium saucepan. Stir over low heat until the sugar has dissolved. Bring the syrup to the boil, then simmer over medium-low heat for 10 minutes, or until it turns a pale caramel colour. Add the remaining ingredients, and continue to simmer until the syrup has reduced by half. Strain and allow to cool slightly before serving.

LIME AND PHILLY PUDDING WITH
ORANGE CARAMEL SAUCE

PASSIONFRUIT AND HAZELNUT TART

MANGO MERINGUE ROLL

PASSIONFRUIT AND HAZELNUT TART

PREPARATION TIME: 40 MINUTES
COOKING TIME: 40 MINUTES
SERVES: 8

1	cup (125g) plain flour
1/2	cup (60g) cornflour
1/4	teaspoon baking powder
1/4	cup ground hazelnuts
125g	butter, chilled and cubed
1/3	cup (75g) caster sugar
1	egg, lightly beaten
250g	block PHILADELPHIA Cream Cheese, softened
2/3	cup (150g) caster sugar
1	cup (250ml) cream
3	eggs, lightly beaten
	grated rind and juice of 1 lemon
1	tablespoon plain flour
1/3	cup fresh passionfruit pulp
	pure cream, to serve
	fresh passionfruit pulp, extra, to serve

SIFT together the plain flour, cornflour and baking powder, and stir through the ground hazelnuts. Rub in the butter until the mixture resembles fine breadcrumbs. Stir in the sugar and enough egg to form a dough. Knead lightly until smooth, shape into a disc, cover with plastic wrap and refrigerate for 30 minutes or until firm.

ROLL the pastry between two sheets of baking paper until large enough to line a 35cm x 10cm rectangular springform tin, or 25cm springform flan tin. Lift the pastry into tin, gently ease into sides and trim the edges neatly. Refrigerate until firm. Prick the pastry lightly with a fork, and cover carefully with baking paper and pastry weights, or dried beans. Bake for 8–10 minutes at 200°C or until just golden. Remove the baking paper and weights and allow to cool.

BEAT the Philly and sugar until smooth. Add combined cream, eggs, lemon rind and juice. Gently stir in the flour and the passionfruit. Pour into prepared shell and bake at 180°C for 20–30 minutes or until set. Serve warm or cold, with a dollop of pure cream and extra passionfruit pulp.

MANGO MERINGUE ROLL

PREPARATION TIME: 20 MINUTES
COOKING TIME: 12–15 MINUTES
SERVES: 4

5	egg whites
1	cup (225g) caster sugar
1	tablespoon cinnamon sugar
1/2	cup (80g) slivered almonds
250g	PHILADELPHIA Spreadable Cream Cheese
2	tablespoons honey
425g	can mango slices, drained, or fresh if available
	pulp of 2 passionfruit
	fresh passionfruit pulp, to serve

LINE a 25cm x 30cm Swiss roll pan with baking paper.

BEAT the egg whites in a large bowl with an electric mixer until stiff (but not dry) peaks form. Add the sugar, 1 tablespoon at a time, beating until the mixture is thick and the sugar has dissolved. Spoon into the lined pan and sprinkle with cinnamon sugar and almonds.

BAKE at 180°C for 12–15 minutes, or until firm to touch. Cool in the pan, then turn the meringue out onto a large sheet of baking paper. Carefully remove the baking paper.

MIX the Philly and honey in a small bowl, then spread over the meringue base. Top with mango slices and passionfruit. Roll up from the short end, as for a Swiss roll, to enclose the filling. Refrigerate to firm. Serve thickly sliced with fresh passionfruit pulp.

APPLE, WALNUT AND BLUEBERRY TART

PREPARATION TIME: 15 MINUTES
COOKING TIME: 1½ HOURS
SERVES: 8

200g shortbread biscuits
 90g (¾ cup) walnuts
 80g butter, melted
  1   medium green apple, finely sliced
  1   punnet (150g) blueberries
 ¼   cup (30g) walnuts, extra, roughly chopped
      double cream, to serve

FILLING

250g block PHILADELPHIA Cream Cheese, softened
  1   cup (225g) caster sugar
 ¾   cup (185ml) cream
      grated rind and juice of 1 orange
 ½   cup (60g) cornflour
 1¼   cups (150g) walnuts, extra, finely chopped

IN a food processor, process the shortbread and walnuts until finely chopped. Add the butter and mix to combine. Press the mixture into the base and sides of a 26cm fluted flan tin. Refrigerate until firm.

SPOON the filling into the prepared crumb crust. Top with the sliced apple, blueberries and extra walnuts.

BAKE at 160°C for 1¼–1½ hours, or until the filling is firm and set in the centre. Serve warm or cold with double cream.

FILLING

BEAT the Philly and sugar with an electric mixer until smooth. Add the cream, orange rind and juice and beat until thick and smooth. Fold in the cornflour and walnuts.

APPLE, WALNUT AND BLUEBERRY TART

THREE CHOCOLATE TERRINE

PREPARATION TIME: 20 MINUTES
REFRIGERATION TIME: 1 HOUR
SERVES: 12

    2   250g blocks PHILADELPHIA Cream cheese, softened
  1/4   cup (55g) caster sugar
    2   teaspoons instant coffee, dissolved
        in 1/4 cup boiling water, cooled
    3   teaspoons gelatine, dissolved in 1/4 cup boiling
        water, cooled
310ml   (1 1/4 cups) cream, whipped
  150g dark cooking chocolate melts
  150g milk cooking chocolate melts
  150g white cooking chocolate melts
        drinking chocolate, to garnish

LINE a 8cm x 22cm loaf pan with plastic wrap and chill.

BEAT the Philly and sugar with an electric mixer until
smooth. Fold through the coffee, gelatine mixture and
whipped cream.

MELT the dark chocolate in a small bowl. When the
chocolate is cool but flowing, fold into one third of the
Philly mixture. Pour into the chilled prepared pan and
refrigerate for 5 minutes or until lightly set.

REPEAT the method for the remaining milk and white
chocolate layers.

REFRIGERATE for one hour or until set. Serve sliced,
dusted with drinking chocolate.

PHILLY COFFEE MOUSSE

PREPARATION TIME: 15 MINUTES
REFRIGERATION TIME: 2 HOURS
MAKES: 6

    2   tablespoons instant coffee granules
 1 1/2 teaspoons gelatine
  1/2   cup (125ml) boiling water
  125g block PHILADELPHIA Cream Cheese, softened
  1/3   cup (75g) caster sugar
  2/3   cup (165ml) cream
    2   eggs
    1   tablespoon coffee liqueur, optional
        coffee beans, to garnish

COMBINE the coffee, gelatine and boiling water in a small
bowl. Whisk with a fork until the gelatine is dissolved. Cool
to room temperature.

BEAT the Philly and sugar in a bowl with an electric mixer
until smooth. Gradually add the cream and eggs; beat until
well combined. Whisk in the coffee mixture and liqueur.

POUR the mixture into 6 x 1/2 cup (125ml) serving dishes
and refrigerate for several hours, or overnight, until set.
Garnish with coffee beans, if desired.

THREE CHOCOLATE TERRINE

PHILLY COFFEE MOUSSE

TERRY'S CHOCOLATE ORANGE CUPCAKES

PREPARATION TIME: 30 MINUTES
COOKING TIME: 15 MINUTES
REFRIGERATION TIME: 10 MINUTES
MAKES: 12

1 1/2 cups sweet biscuit crumbs
80g butter, melted
3 250g blocks PHILADELPHIA Cream Cheese, softened
3/4 cup (165g) caster sugar
1/4 cup (60ml) cream
2 eggs, lightly beaten
grated rind and juice of 1 orange
1 1/2 tablespoons cornflour
2 40g Terry's Chocolate Orange Bars, chopped
1 tablespoon (20g) butter, extra

COMBINE the biscuit crumbs and butter. Press into the lined 12 x 1/2 cup (125ml) capacity non-stick muffin pan and chill until firm.

BEAT the Philly and the sugar in an electric mixer until just combined. Beat in the cream, egg, orange juice and rind. Gently stir in the cornflour. Pour the mixture into prepared pans and bake at 160°C for 15 minutes or until just set. Allow to cool.

COMBINE Terry's Chocolate Orange Bars and extra butter over low heat until smooth. Drizzle muffins with topping and chill until set.

ROCKY ROAD CHEESECAKE

PREPARATION TIME: 25 MINUTES
REFRIGERATION TIME: 2 HOURS
SERVES: 10

1 1/4 cups chocolate biscuit crumbs
1/4 cup (25g) desiccated coconut
1/4 cup KRAFT Crunchy Peanut Butter
60g butter, melted
2 250g blocks PHILADELPHIA Cream Cheese, softened
1/4 cup (55g) caster sugar
200g milk cooking chocolate melts, melted
1/2 cup (125ml) cream
2 teaspoons gelatine dissolved in
1/4 cup (60ml) boiling water, cooled
2 cups (170g) white and pink marshmallows, halved
1/2 cup (100g) red glacé cherries, chopped

COMBINE the biscuit crumbs, coconut, peanut butter and butter in a small bowl. Press the mixture into base of a 22cm springform pan lined with baking paper. Chill in the freezer for 10 minutes.

BEAT the Philly and sugar in a large bowl with an electric mixer until smooth. Add the melted chocolate, cream and gelatine mixture and beat until combined. Stir in the marshmallows and cherries.

POUR the mixture into the crumb crust and chill for 2 hours, or until set.

TERRY'S CHOCOLATE ORANGE CUPCAKES

ROCKY ROAD CHEESECAKE

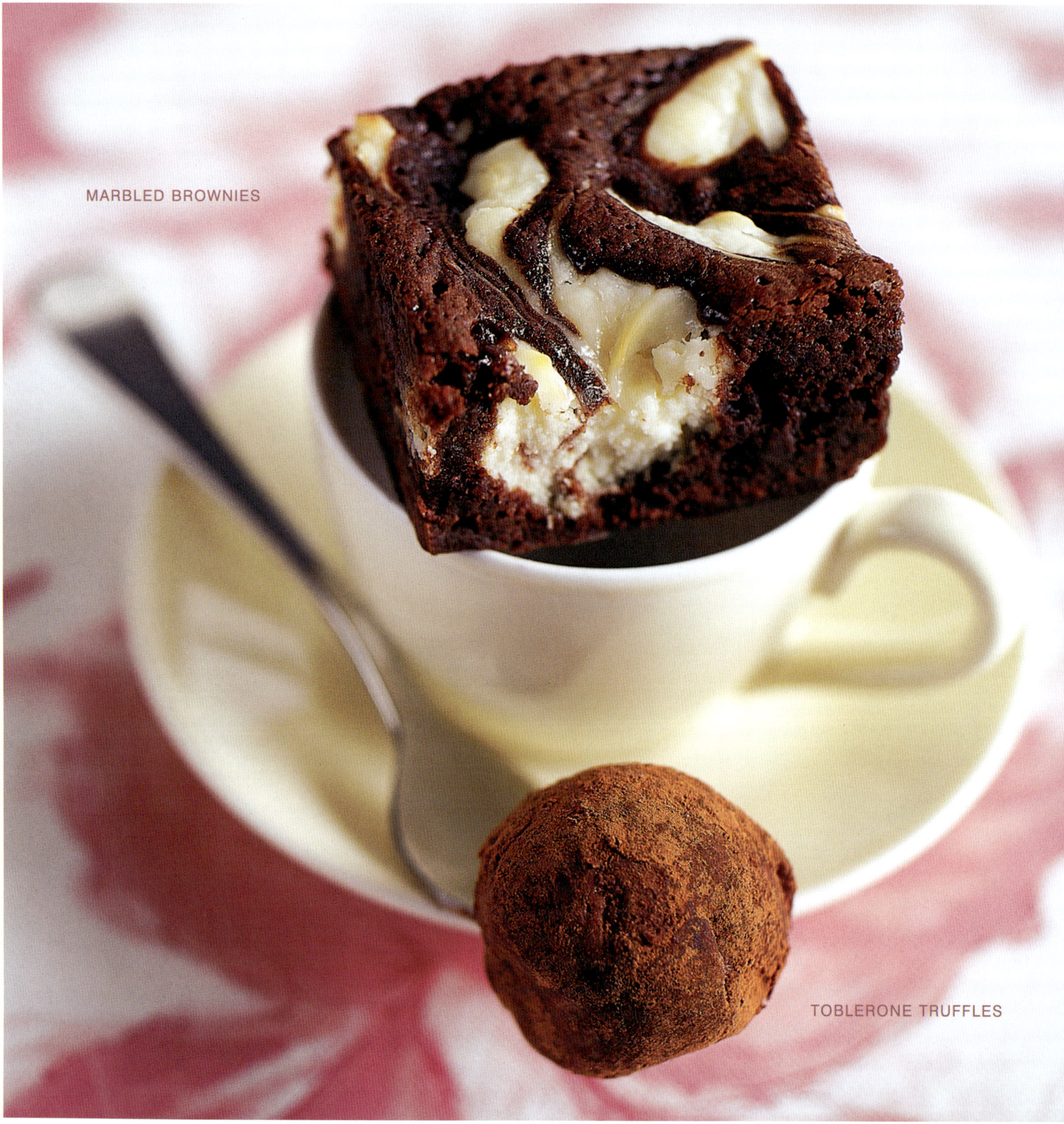

MARBLED BROWNIES

TOBLERONE TRUFFLES

MARBLED BROWNIES

PREPARATION TIME: 20 MINUTES
COOKING TIME: 40 MINUTES
MAKES: 20

125g butter
125g dark chocolate, chopped
   1 cup (250g) brown sugar, lightly packed
   3 eggs, lightly beaten
 1/3 cup (40g) plain flour, sifted
 1/3 cup (40g) cocoa powder
 1/4 teaspoon baking powder
250g Light PHILADELPHIA Spreadable
      Cream Cheese, softened
 1/4 cup (55g) caster sugar

LIGHTLY grease a 16cm x 26cm slab tin and line the base
with baking paper.

COMBINE the butter, chocolate and brown sugar in a
medium saucepan. Stir over moderate heat until the
chocolate and butter have melted. Remove from heat and
whisk in the eggs. Stir in the sifted flour, cocoa and baking
powder until well combined and pour into prepared pan.

MIX the Philly and the sugar in a small bowl until smooth.
Spoon it randomly over chocolate mixture and swirl to mix
with the tip of a knife. Bake at 180°C for 35–40 minutes
(loosely cover with foil if over-browning).

KRAFT KITCHENS HANDY HINT

BROWNIES have a soft fudgy texture. The top should appear
firm, and when tested with a skewer, a few moist crumbs
should stick.

TOBLERONE TRUFFLES

PREPARATION TIME: 30 MINUTES
REFRIGERATION TIME: 1 HOUR
MAKES: 24

250g block PHILADELPHIA Cream Cheese, softened
   2 tablespoons sour cream
   1 tablespoon honey
   1 tablespoon amaretto, optional
100g dark Toblerone, melted
 1/4 cup (40g) chopped almonds, toasted
      cocoa, sifted, for rolling

BEAT the Philly, sour cream, honey and amaretto with an
electric mixer in a small bowl until light and creamy. Fold
in the melted chocolate and almonds.

REFRIGERATE until firm (about 1 hour). Shape into
tablespoon-sized balls and roll in cocoa. Refrigerate the
truffles until they are required.

MIDDLE EASTERN
BOILED FRUIT CAKE

PREPARATION TIME: 20 MINUTES
COOKING TIME: 1 HOUR
SERVES: 10–12

250g block Light PHILADELPHIA Cream Cheese, softened
200g (1²/3 cups) sultanas
200g (1²/3 cups) raisins, chopped
100g (¹/2 cup) Turkish apricots, chopped
100g (¹/2 cup) pitted dates, chopped
100g (¹/2 cup) dried figs, chopped
150g (1 cup) blanched almonds
 85g (²/3 cup) shelled pistachios
 90g (¹/2 cup) brown sugar, lightly packed
 50g (1 cup) flaked coconut
   2 teaspoons cinnamon
1¹/2 teaspoons nutmeg
   1 teaspoon bicarbonate of soda
   1 cup (250ml) water
   1 teaspoon rose water
   2 eggs, lightly beaten
   1 cup (125g) plain flour, sifted
 ¹/2 cup (60g) self-raising flour, sifted
   1 cup (250g) sugar
   1 cup (250ml) water
   2 cups mixed dried fruits and nuts
      rosebuds, optional, to garnish

COMBINE the Philly, fruit, nuts, sugar, coconut, spices, bicarbonate of soda, water and rose water in a saucepan. Bring the mixture to the boil, stirring, then allow to cool.

ADD the eggs and mix well. Stir in the sifted flours until combined.

POUR the batter into a 24cm springform pan, lined with baking paper.

BAKE at 160°C for 40–50 minutes, or until a skewer inserted into the centre comes out clean.

COMBINE the sugar and water in a small saucepan, over medium heat until the sugar dissolves. Add the mixed fruits and nuts and simmer for 20 minutes, or until the syrup thickens. Pour over the cake and garnish with rosebuds.

STORE in an airtight container for up to 2 weeks.

MIDDLE EASTERN
BOILED FRUIT CAKE

chef profiles

As you made your way through the recipe section of this book, you will have found twelve Philly recipes featuring restaurant logos. The following talented chefs generously supplied their inspiration for those pages. We took a little time out of their busy schedules to chat to them about themselves, and their businesses.

OWEN LACEY

Circā

483 ADELAIDE
STREET, BRISBANE,
QUEENSLAND

Canadian born and New Zealand raised Owen Lacey, rose to prominence as a young chef representing New Zealand in the Amsterdam Culinary Olympics. He travelled to Australia in 1993, working in many of our top restaurants, finally settling at Circa as Sous Chef, under Craig Hopson. Taking full advantage of Craig's tutelage – and 3 star Michelin training – Owen was able to step up into the role as Chef de Cuisine in February 2001.

Since his appointment, Circa has been merited with the awards 'Restaurant of the Year 2001' and 'Best Fine Dining, Queensland 2001'. He was also honoured to be invited to participate in the 'Centenary of Federation Dinner' with two other well-known practitioners of Modern Australian Cuisine, Janni Kyritsis of MG Garage NSW and Neal Jackson of Jacksons WA.

For the curious, a visit to Circa reveals a contemporary space in a 100-year-old warehouse, overlooking the Brisbane River. Owen and his team can be sighted bustling away in the open kitchen producing seasonal Australian dishes with a 'French twist'.

SHIRLEY DOUGLAS

Tall Timbers

SCOTCHTOWN ROAD,
SMITHTON, TASMANIA

Cable Beach International Broome, Jupiters Casino, The Whitsundays, Port Douglas, Fraser Island, Kakadu and Tasmania – Shirley Douglas' resume reads like the dream Aussie holiday itinerary. Her 15 years in the industry have found her at some of Australia's best noted and picturesque resorts giving her a grounding in catering for both the masses and the more intimate occasions.

You will currently find Shirley at Tall Timbers resort in Smithton Tasmania, a 165-acre lush and rustic setting. Well known in the local Tourism Industry as a celebration of natural heritage and the Tasmanian pioneering spirit, Tall Timbers has been a consistent winner of tourism awards and recently claimed the prize of AHA Best Bistro.

Featuring on the property is a well stocked trout stream – and as Tassie is amply equipped with some of the best produce in Australia – Shirley has at her fingertips an array of the finest local foods with which to tantalise the many international tourists that visit the resort. To fill this role, she is naturally a very passionate and driven individual – with very high and exacting standards. She maintains the integrity of her menus by making everything from scratch – from the stock to the baked items.

ARNI SLEEMAN

La Linea

92B ACLAND STREET
ST KILDA, VICTORIA

Arni Sleeman was until recently the chef and co-owner of Punch Lane, the well known, award-winning Melbourne wine bar and restaurant. His new venture, La Linea, in the heart of vibrant Acland Street, St.Kilda, is a sharply designed mecca for lovers of simply executed, inspirational Italian food, in a bustling and cosmopolitan hub.

Beginning his career in the 1980s at Fleurie, he rose to the position of Sous Chef at a time when Fleurie was awarded three chef's hats in *The Age Good Food Guide*. In 1987 Arni became Head Chef at the innovative and popular South Melbourne restaurant, The Last Aussie Fishcaf – also functioning as Executive Head Chef at The Last Aussie Fishcaf's two sister restaurants in Sydney and on the Gold Coast.

In 1992, a move to London saw him surface as Sous Chef at the De Lugo Bar Café Restaurant, under Antony Worrel Thompson. He then moved on to 190 Queens Gate – the restaurant at Kensington's Gore Hotel – nominated as Best Restaurant in Lord Litchfield's gourmet food guide, with its downstairs restaurant following up by winning Best Seafood Restaurant.

On his return to Melbourne, he established his own catering business. He then took on the position of Head Chef at Iain Hewitson's Tolarno Bar & Bistro, until establishing the much awarded Punch Lane in 1995, and more recently La Linea, which will branch into a chain of similar restaurants.

IAN CURLEY

THE POINT
ALBERT PARK LAKE

AQUATIC DRIVE,
ALBERT PARK,
VICTORIA

Ian Curley is often referred to by the Australian Food Media as one of the famous 'Brit Pack'. Like culinary stars Jeremy Strode and Donovan Cooke, he began his career in the UK working with the Savoy and Hyatt Groups, eventually making Melbourne his home. On arrival in Australia he lent his touch to the award-winning Rhubarbs and Stella.

In his current role for five years, Ian oversees the kitchens at three spectacular locations: The Point at Albert Park, The Beaumaris Pavillion and The Mentone Hotel. Leading a team of 40 staff, Ian has the rare freedom to produce menus of various styles and to express his ideas across different styles of venues. His efforts have resulted in a Critic's Choice Award from Community Aid Abroad with whom the group have participated in raising funds at Taste's of a Nation. Additionally since 1997, The Point has consistently been awarded 2 hats in *The Age Good Food Guide* and The Beaumaris Pavillion receiving 1 hat in its first year.

To assist the inspirational process, and maintain his culinary edge, Ian has travelled to Singapore and Mauritius to participate in food events. He enjoys the Australian lifestyle and insists on taking the time to keep abreast of culinary trends and demands, in order to challenge and inspire others.

TONY FAZIO

RAGAZZI

165 MILLS STREET,
MIDDLE PARK,
VICTORIA

Ragazzi is well regarded as one of the innovators of the wood fired pizza movement in Melbourne. Often copied, their pizzas have a legion of devoted fans, who have been enjoying the casual ambience of this beachside restaurant for seven years. The loyalty has a lot to do with Tony Fazio's personal philosophy, which basically involves a hands-on approach, getting to know – and understand – his customer's varied tastes and lifestyle.

Cited by The Age's 'Epicure' supplement as one of Melbourne's best pizza venues, Ragazzi began with a largely Italian menu. Some recipes drawing on Tony's family's heritage, others reflecting his training in Italy. Today in response to his clientele, the menus take a broader approach, embracing influences from many cultures. He has his own spin on Mediterranean classics which thrill his guests. The specials menu has evolved over the years, and each month they are themed to reflect a different cuisine such as North African or Oriental.

On summer nights and weekends the whole place is bustling with tanned bodies and enthusiastic staff. You'll find the locals sitting shoulder to shoulder with those who have been recommended by word of mouth – and Tony is there, making sure that everyone feels welcome. In winter, pizza fans warm themselves near the wood stove – for to them, Ragazzi is a comfortable old friend.

MARTIN THOMPSON

CATALINA ROSE BAY

1 SUNDERLAND AVE,
LYNE PARK, ROSE BAY,
NEW SOUTH WALES

With 15 years in the industry, Martin Thompson is a Baker, in heart and soul. He came to Australia five years ago from the UK, after hearing rave reviews of the great Australian lifestyle, the fresh produce and innovative cuisine. Inspired by a childhood spent watching Mum baking Blueberry pies, he found himself working at the Atlantic Bar & Grill in London, then moving on to De Lugo with Anthony Worrel Thompson.

In Australia he opened Fuel in Surrey Hills and supplied Prunier and Belmondo, amongst many well known Sydney restaurants, with pastries & baked goods. Tired of the exhausting hours required in his own business, he took on a position at the famous Bayswater Brasserie. Now, the position at Catalina, sees him complementing Angel Fenandez's inspirational dishes with his sweet delights.

Overlooking the sweep of Rose Bay, the stunning Catalina is rated 2 hats by *The Sydney Morning Herald Good Food Guide*. With slick modern décor, and a breathtaking panorama, it's a regular watering hole for celebrities and a popular venue for weddings, giving Martin the pleasure of producing sumptuously beautiful wedding cakes. Still passionate about his baking, he describes his style as classic, and ensures that his sour dough is created with fresh organic produce. Unlike many others in the business, Martin still loves to cook at home rather than venture out.

MATT GOLINSKI

RICKY RICARDO'S

NOOSA WHARF,
QUAMBY PLACE,
NOOSA HEADS,
QUEENSLAND

The team at Ricky Ricardo's feel that they are very much a family. Chef Matt Golinski joined Leonie Palmer & Stef Fisher's team at their Noosa icon nearly 3 years ago, after extensive and inspirational travel through Asia, Europe and North Africa. A Sunshine Coast native he loves the intimacy of the setting and the joy of bringing new and exotic innovations to their clientele. As an advocate of local, organic and chemical-free foods, Matt's dishes constantly challenge the palates of regulars – who claim Ricky Rickardo's as their second home.

The style of their menus is largely Mediterranean with an accent of Middle Eastern and North African styles. Leonie describes it as "a colourful cuisine touched by the sun", as showcased in her book, Leonie Palmer's *Noosa Cookbook*. Touched by the sun is also appropriate to the setting. Ricky Rickardo's features a delightful deck jutting over the water, where guests arriving by boat can be viewed and special occasions are highlighted by spectacular sunsets. Rated the Best Sunshine Coast Restaurant by American Express, and featuring in most of Australia's better known food guides, Ricky Ricardo's service and quality stand testament to its popularity with tourists and locals alike.

LORETTA SARTORI

Distorta

P.O. BOX 1069,
COLLINGWOOD,
VICTORIA

Although described as the Principessa of Dolce and Diva of the Dessert by her peers, Loretta Sartori once wanted to be a cook. She left school to work in the business now well known to Melbourne cake lovers as Brunetti, but moved on to work with Melbourne restaurant icon Tony Rogalsky. After 2 weeks, she had realised her mistake. Her passion was for pastry. She moved on to Arnold's Swiss Cakes and later went to train under Joel Bellouet in Paris.

Fascinated by the technical, and the formulas involved in her art, Loretta is not only a fantastic Pastry Chef, but also a gifted teacher. For many years she held classes at Diane Holuigue's cooking school, The French Kitchen – an institution that brought the finer points of the culinary arts into many homes. Her fans have since followed her to Master Class presentations at The Melbourne Food and Wine Festival, and at the Cooking Schools of The Melbourne Hilton, The Vital Ingredient and The Victoria Market.

In 1996 she opened Distorta Designer Cakes, which deservedly has a huge following in the Hospitality Industry. Her dazzling creations are now baked to order for special occasions for clients such as The Hilton, The Windsor, The Marriott, Epicure Catering, and Peter Rowland Catering. She has also found time to collaborate with Stephano Di Pieri on the delightful cookbook *A Gondola On The Murray*.

MARTIN WALKER

bluestone

349 FLINDERS LANE,
MELBOURNE,
VICTORIA

Love brought Martin Walker to Australia. Originally from the UK, he met his Australian wife on the snowfields of Austria. The rest as they say, is history. With a background of chefing with The Savoy Group and Spencer House Corporate Catering, he also participated in a number of celebrated food events. To his credit were the catering of the GAT talks in London, The Queen Mother's Birthday Celebrations, and the Henley Regatta.

In Melbourne, he joined the much awarded restaurant at The Adelphi Hotel, which at the time, enjoyed 2 chef's hats in *The Age Good Food Guide*. Martin has also worked at the popular Halcyon Restaurant in Toorak and the legendary Chinois Deux, where amongst many A-list functions, he created a dazzling launch party for Cartier.

Today, in the heart of the business district of inner city Melbourne, he is teamed with his old partner from Chinois Deux, Mickael Gaultier at Bluestone Restaurant and Bar. French influenced Modern European cuisine is the core focus for the team – the perfect venue for those as serious about their food as their business. Bluestone walls and rich furnishings make time here an elegant diversion from the working day. Downstairs, the setting is more informal, servicing city dwellers and workers with a café and lounge bar for evening revellers.

JIM FRANGOS

FRANGOS&FRANGOS

82 VINCENT STREET
DAYLESFORD,
VICTORIA

The Frangos family have been involved in food and hospitality since the extended families arrival in Australia in the 1920s. Jim grew up in and around the extended family businesses which ranged from restaurants and cafés to provedores. Likewise, his daughters Petra and Melia have grown up on barstools and in the kitchens of his ventures.

Today Jim and daughter Melia have a hands-on approach to Daylesford's Frangos & Frangos, in the heart of Victoria's Spa District. The region is well known for its Swiss-Italian heritage and consequently the plethora of specialist gourmet products, wine and organic produce available, are showcased. Housed in a great old building, the business is split between a wellness centre, Frangos & Frangos restaurant and Koukla Pizzeria which features wood fired delights.

Attracting many tourists, Frangos & Frangos has been featured in nearly every one of Australia's gourmet guides and has been well reviewed in the food media. To Jim's credit F&F has been consistently nominated for the American Express Best Restaurant Award. His team in the kitchen have varied experience, with stints at the famous Jean Jacques, Mink Bar at the Prince of Wales, and Warrrenmang Winery.

PETER EVANS

Hugo's

70 CAMPBELL PDE,
BONDI BEACH,
NEW SOUTH WALES

Completing his apprenticeship as a chef in Melbourne at the age of 20, Peter's first appointment as a head chef was at The Pantry in Brighton. Six months later he became a financial partner and expanded the business with a catering division.

Moving to Sydney in 1996 Peter established his second restaurant Hugo's in Bondi. Hugo's received a Sydney Morning Herald chef's hat in 1999, 2000 and 2001. The teams' hands-on approach has given their restaurants a reputation for excellent food in a fun and friendly environment. Local and international celebrities recognise Hugo's as an institution; a "must do" on the Sydney social circuit and its success relies heavily on its reputation of fine food and friendly, professional and caring staff.

The team recently opened Hugo's Lounge, a fine dining restaurant with soft lounges, soft music and beautiful food situated in Kings Cross. Peter and Manu Feildel (head chef from Live Bait in London) combine their talents to produce an excellent blend of French and Modern Australian Cuisine. This year Peter is forming Hugo's Catering in Sydney and developing a cookbook showcasing an in-depth look at his food, recipes and restaurants. He is also cooking up a storm on The LifeStyle Channel's Home series and contributing recipes to publications such as Australian Table.

Index